Governing Social Virtual Reality

Joanne E. Gray · Marcus Carter · Ben Egliston

Governing Social Virtual Reality

Preparing for the Content, Conduct and Design Challenges of Immersive Social Media

palgrave
macmillan

Joanne E. Gray
University of Sydney
Sydney, NSW, Australia

Marcus Carter
University of Sydney
Sydney, NSW, Australia

Ben Egliston
University of Sydney
Sydney, NSW, Australia

ISBN 978-3-031-61833-8 ISBN 978-3-031-61831-4 (eBook)
https://doi.org/10.1007/978-3-031-61831-4

This Palgrave Macmillan imprint is published by the registered company Springer Nature Switzerland AG
The registered company address is: Gewerbestrasse 11, 6330 Cham, Switzerland

Acknowledgements

The work that informs this book is partly based on research projects funded by TikTok Pte. Ltd. and Meta Platforms Inc. We sincerely appreciate their support for our work. We are also grateful to Palgrave and the Pivot series for supporting this kind of knowledge production, a short and rapidly published book that can provide regulators, policymakers and technology platforms a baseline from which to begin or improve the governance of VR, something we believe is not just good for users but also for the wider adoption and success of immersive technologies.

Contents

Abbreviations

AR	Augmented Reality
MR	Mixed Reality
VR	Virtual Reality
XR	Extended Reality

PART I

What Needs Governing?

CHAPTER 1

Introduction

Abstract This chapter summarises the benefits, risks of harm and other complexities presented by social virtual reality (VR), and the need for proactive governance and regulation. It emphasises that immersion in VR can amplify the intensity of user experiences, both positive and negative, underscoring the need for a nuanced approach to content moderation and inclusive design practices. The chapter sets forth the key aims of this book, which includes equipping industry leaders and policymakers with the knowledge required for proactive social VR governance, ensuring equitable safety and success for all users.

Keywords Virtual reality · Content harms · Regulation · Content moderation · Immersive environments · Inclusive design · Platform governance

In our teaching, we have had more than 1000 students experience virtual reality (VR) for the very first time. It is an unusual teaching experience: a busy computer lab, in which 20 students are blind to the physical classroom and transport themselves to a completely new, virtual space. Nearly all of them will forget, for a moment, where they are as they become fully immersed in VR. We show students VR films so realistic and immersive that they nod their heads when the actor speaks to the camera, as though

J. E. Gray et al., *Governing Social Virtual Reality*,
https://doi.org/10.1007/978-3-031-61831-4_1

they are really speaking to them.[1] We let them explore *Google Earth* in VR and watch as most travel not to tourist landmarks, but nostalgically revisit their childhood home or other places to which they feel connected. Most importantly, we let them play: sculpting 3D artwork in *TiltBrush*, chasing a mouse through a forest in *Moss*, controlling time with their bodies in *Super Hot VR* and dispatching dozens of enemies in *Bullet Train*. When we finally pull them out from their virtual universes at the end of the lesson, we ask them to pay close attention to their bodies, noticing how their heart rate is elevated from the very real, virtual excitement.

As critical as we are in this book and other research about VR and its potential for harm, we are also excited about this technology, because we see in our students how powerful and valuable immersive experiences can be. When embodied in a virtual space, people can experience a profound sense of connection with the worlds they encounter. Social VR—where multiple people are occupying a shared virtual space at once—offers an opportunity for connection, immersion and togetherness that flat, 2D social media simply cannot provide. It is one of this decade's most exciting technological frontiers.

These same affordances, however, can also amplify the risks and consequences of harmful experiences. Once you feel embodied in VR—when it feels like your virtual body *is* your physical body—actions taken against that body feel real. In a digital game, this can be an attractive experience, enabling thrilling first-person shooter experiences or haunting horror games. In social VR, however, unwanted feelings of bodily threat can quickly become harmful harassment or assault. This book explores these issues, specifically examining the potential for both *content* and *conduct* harms, data harms, barriers to accessibility by diverse VR users and the safety implications presented by the participation of children within social VR environments.

The primary focus of the book is social VR, that is, multi-user VR environments. Currently, these are most prominently leisure-based social platforms—including, for example, *Horizon Worlds, RecRoom* and *VRChat*—but VR is also used in multiplayer games and, in the near future, we can expect it to be integrated into workplaces through platforms such as Microsoft Teams. Consistent with industry and academic definitions, we understand VR as denoting immersive, completely digital, or simulated experiences reliant on head-mounted displays. At times in this book, we also refer to extended reality (XR) because it has emerged as a preferred term in much of the recent policy discourse concerning VR.

XR is an umbrella term that describes a spectrum of digital technologies that incorporate the spatial dimensions of the digital into the physical and vice versa. XR includes VR, augmented reality (AR) and mixed reality (MR)—what Apple Inc. prefers to call 'spatial computing'. All of these technologies share a suite of governance challenges.

Like social media, the content that can be created, shared and interacted within social VR may harm users. This is a well-known platform governance problem: platforms must determine what is acceptable content for their community of users. However, given VR's immersive nature, the impact of exposure to harmful materials—such as harassment, violence or sexually explicit content—has the potential to be more profound than on 2D platforms. In recent years, various incidents in social VR have underscored this concern, including representations of suicide and recreations of mass shootings. Social VR platforms require decisive content moderation strategies to safeguard users from content harms.

Social VR also introduces the governance challenge of moderating user *conduct*. In a significant departure from text and image-centric digital media, VR includes spatial and temporal affordances, offering spaces where users can communicate through the behaviour of avatars. Typically, social VR interfaces include voice and gaze interaction, motion controls and body-tracking, all of which foster a heightened sense of presence. Such features can be conduits for harm when they enable, for example, unwanted avatar contact, stalking or offensive gestures. As we detail in this book, research suggests that harassment is already extremely common in social VR. Users have reported cases of sexual assault, racial abuse, homophobic slurs and death threats. The embodied nature of VR, the synchronicity of interactions and the perception of shared physical space can all serve to intensify the psychological impact of these experiences.

Successfully moderating both content and conduct in social VR environments requires a multidimensional approach. We argue that this must include both *reactive* and *proactive* measures. Reactive measures, such as user reporting, should work in tandem with proactive measures, like personal boundaries, to prevent harm. That is, VR must be *designed* to be safe and equitable for diverse cohorts of users. Automated moderation systems that utilise machine learning can be used to oversee social spaces for potential rule violations, but human moderation is critical for identifying the contextual nuances of harmful conduct and content in social VR. Human and community moderation, facilitated by platform tools for enforcement, can play an important role in fostering a pro-social platform culture.

As social VR continues to advance, a proactive, multidimensional approach to VR platform design and governance will be essential for creating inclusive virtual spaces in which the rights and needs of all participants are respected. In the spirit of the Palgrave Pivot series, the purpose of this book is to begin defining a pathway towards achieving this goal and use the rapid publication model to intervene in the global regulatory and policy debates today. Such an initiative is crucial because these conversations need to take place *now*, before the technology becomes entrenched in inequitable and otherwise harmful ways. As our book goes on to account, there are available sufficient insights from established academic research to begin taking these steps.

Broadly speaking, our book is divided into two parts. Part I, comprising Chapters 1–4, explores *what* needs governing in social VR, covering content, conduct and young people. In Part II, comprising Chapters 5–8, we turn to the question of *how* to achieve good governance, including principles, current practices and regulation by government.

Chapter 2 outlines how harmful content, including hate speech, misinformation, conspiracy theories and ideologically driven violence, can be intensified in social VR environments. Drawing from examples across different social VR platforms, the chapter discusses the difficulty of content moderation in VR and the potential for real-world harm. It explores the applicability of existing online content-harm mitigation approaches, such as community guidelines and automated moderation, to social VR, highlighting the unique challenges posed by the immersive nature of VR. The chapter concludes by addressing the future complexities of harmful content in MR and AR environments, stressing the importance of context-aware human moderation, AI support and the cultivation of pro-social community norms to prevent content harms.

Chapter 3 delves into the complexities of conduct harms in social VR, emphasising the distinctive challenges posed by VR's spatial and temporal affordances which can intensify experiences of harassment, particularly 'embodied harassment'. The chapter highlights the inadequacy of current moderation practices and the unique forms of gender-based harm prevalent within VR environments. It critiques the current reliance on reactive safety features, which often fail to protect users effectively, and underscores the necessity for a more proactive approach to governance and policymaking. By examining the psychological and social impacts of conduct harms, the chapter calls for a reevaluation of community norms and the development of more inclusive and effective moderation tools, advocating for a synergy between human, automated and community-based approaches to ensure user safety in social VR platforms.

In Chapter 4, we explore the multifaceted impacts of social VR on children, focusing on the potential for physiological, psychological and social harm. The chapter highlights how concerns about children's digital media use, in general, have been applied to VR, particularly the issue of media addiction. It also reviews research on the physiological effects of VR on children's vision and balance, the difficulties that children may have in distinguishing VR from reality and the risk of social harms such as targeted harassment and exposure to mature content. The chapter emphasises the need for robust age-appropriate design, supervision and content moderation to protect young users in VR environments. It also addresses the broader implications of children's presence in social VR spaces for adult users, emphasising the need for community norms that support a safe and inclusive environment for all ages. Taken together, this overview adds to calls against the further expansion of children's use of VR without better research and safeguards.

Turning to how we might govern social VR given the issues examined in part one of the book, in Chapter 5, we address the imperative of designing social VR environments with safety, privacy and inclusivity at the forefront. We explain the privacy concerns posed by biometric and spatial data collection in VR, emphasising the need for continuous consent and informed user choices. We also critique the gendered and ableist biases in current VR design. We advocate for prioritising accessibility in VR development through the inclusion of disabled users in design processes as well as better representations of disabilities in avatars. Finally, we discuss design considerations for children, including age-gating and parental controls. The overarching theme of this chapter is the ethical responsibility of VR developers to design environments and devices that are safe and inclusive for all users.

Chapter 6 adds to our understanding of this responsibility via a review of the spectrum of moderation techniques currently deployed across social VR platforms to tackle user conduct and content issues, distinguishing between reactive and proactive strategies. We evaluate common reactive safety features like in-app reporting, vote kicking, blocking and user monitoring, noting their limitations and the burden they place on victims. The chapter also explores proactive measures, including personal boundaries and voice controls. It underscores the importance of a multifaceted approach to platform governance that combines both reactive and proactive elements aimed at fostering pro-social behaviours and community norms.

Chapter 7 examines the evolving landscape of social VR regulations, emphasising the need for government intervention to ensure that VR environments are safe, trustworthy and equitable. It discusses a variety of regulatory approaches, from varying jurisdictions, including soft law proposals such as best practice principles and industry codes of conduct, highlighting the current collaborative efforts of civil society groups, government and industry stakeholders. The chapter critiques existing self-governance initiatives and assesses key legislative initiatives globally, including online safety laws and data regulations. This chapter advocates for proactive regulatory interventions that place obligations on platforms to prevent harms and protect the public interest whilst VR technologies continue to evolve.

In the conclusion to the book, Chapter 8, we synthesise our exploration of social VR platform governance, arguing for inclusive immersive environments in which the rights and needs of all participants are respected. We present five principles essential for achieving this: promoting pro-social cultures, prioritising prevention over reaction, embedding safety by design, ensuring user control and choice and enforcing platform responsibility and accountability. These principles offer a durable framework for addressing social VR's governance challenges amid rapid technological and industry changes, aiming to guide regulators, policymakers and platforms towards safer and more inclusive virtual spaces.

The research that informs the book includes an analysis of existing codes of conduct or community guidelines for multi-user VR environments including *Horizon Worlds*, *RecRoom*, *VR Chat* and *AltspaceVR*; a review of media reportage around VR platforms; an analysis of user discussions about related topics on social VR community forums (specific application forums and Reddit communities) and a comprehensive review of academic literature relating to the topic of VR harms. The book is also informed by a multi-year project by the authors on the ethical implications XR including a 2022 review of corporate, civil society and government XR (or 'metaverse') initiatives and two 2023 studies of the US and Chinese XR economies.

In this book, we have endeavoured to distil current understandings of social VR and the complexities of its oversight into a format that is both digestible and actionable. As the field and industry continue to advance, we expect the specifics of social VR's governance challenges to change. Nonetheless, we are confident that the foundational principles we have established in this book will continue to be relevant as the technology and its use evolve. The book is intended to lay the groundwork for VR's stakeholders—industry, policymakers, regulators—to proactively take up the challenge of governing immersive social media.

Note

1. Carter, M., Webber, S., Rawson, S., Smith, W., Purdam, J., and McLeod, E. "Virtual Reality in the Zoo: A Qualitative Evaluation of a Stereoscopic Virtual Reality Video Encounter with Little Penguins (Eudyptula Minor)." *Journal of Zoo and Aquarium Research* 8, No. 4 (2020): 239–245.

CHAPTER 2

Content Harms in Social VR: Abuse, Misinformation, Platform Cultures and Moderation

Abstract This chapter examines the challenges and implications of content harms within social Virtual Reality (VR) platforms. It outlines how harmful content, including misinformation, conspiracy theories and ideologically driven violence, can be intensified in immersive VR environments. Drawing from examples across different social VR platforms, the chapter discusses the difficulty of content moderation in VR and the potential for real-world harm. It explores the applicability of existing online content-harm mitigation approaches, such as community guidelines and automated moderation, to social VR, highlighting the unique challenges posed by the immersive nature of VR. The chapter concludes by addressing the future complexities of harmful content in mixed and augmented reality environments, stressing the importance of context-aware human moderation, AI support and the cultivation of pro-social community norms to prevent content harm in VR spaces.

Keywords Virtual reality · Content harms · Social virtual reality · Content moderation · Immersive environments · Community guidelines · Pro-social norms · Misinformation in VR · Human vs AI moderation · Content warnings · VR harms · Online communities

J. E. Gray et al., *Governing Social Virtual Reality*,
https://doi.org/10.1007/978-3-031-61831-4_2

Introduction

In 2022, Buzzfeed News journalists conducted an experiment to test Meta's rules against harmful content on its social VR platform *Horizon Worlds*. They set up a private room dubbed 'The Qniverse', based on the QAnon conspiracy.[1] Within the Qniverse, conspiracy theories and misinformation-related phrases floated throughout the virtual space, including 'Stop the Plandemic!', 'Stop the Steal!' and 'where we go one we go all', a notorious QAnon slogan. The space also featured a looped soundtrack of *Inforwars* host, Alex Jones, calling US President Joe Biden a paedophile and proclaiming that reptilian humanoids rigged the 2020 US presidential elections. Essentially, the Qniverse was an immersive revelry of the QAnon conspiracy theory.

Adherents to QAnon believe in the existence of a global satanic paedophile ring—comprising powerful figures entrenched within the US government and industry—and that former US President Donald Trump is covertly waging a war against it. Despite the outlandish nature of the theory and a complete lack of evidence to support it, QAnon has radicalised vast numbers of individuals and spurred numerous acts of real-world violence within the United States, where authorities categorise it as a domestic terror threat.[2]

The first act of violence directly tied to QAnon—colloquially referred to as 'pizzagate'—occurred in 2016 when an email from a Hillary Clinton staffer was leaked to the public and interpreted by QAnon adherents as containing coded messages and satanic symbols, allegedly revealing a child sex trafficking operation in a Washington D.C. pizza restaurant. This resulted in ongoing harassment of the restaurant's workers and, in December 2016, a man armed with a handgun and assault rifle fired multiple shots at the building, demanding access to investigate the premises. Numerous violent incidents involving individuals claiming to be motivated by QAnon have occurred since.

As part of Meta's Dangerous Individuals and Organisations policy, first introduced by the company in 2021, *Horizon Worlds* has rules against content association with movements and organisations linked to violence.[3] Buzzfeed's Qniverse was clearly in violation of this policy. However, when Buzzfeed alerted *Horizon Worlds* moderators to the existence of the Qniverse by using the platform's reporting system, it was deemed compliant with the company's rules and no action was taken.

The Qniverse was only removed from *Horizon Worlds* when Buzzfeed reached out to Meta's public relations team for comment.

Whilst the Qniverse was experimental—designed to test Meta's content moderation policies—it demonstrates how social VR platforms have the potential to worsen existing digital platform problems that harm societies and individuals. Over the past decade, social media has played a pivotal role in the propagation and consolidation of misinformation and conspiracy theories. Studies show how QAnon followers, for example, use platforms such as Facebook, Parler, Twitter, 4Chan, Reddit, Gab and Telegram to connect, share information and recruit new members through social processes of meaning-making. As Marwick et al. (2022) explain, QAnon has been fuelled by "collective knowledge-making activity built on the affordances of social media designed to construct specific facts and theories that maintain QAnon's cohesion over time".[4] Indicatively, in 2022, the UN's Office of Counter-Terrorism and Violent Extremism's expert panel on *Safeguarding the Metaverse: Countering Terrorism and Preventing Violent Extremism in Digital Space* identified terrorist recruitment as a critical future issue for VR.[5] If social VR platforms' userbases grow and follow the patterns seen in social media over the past decade, the possibility for social VR to be used in ways that result in real-world harm must be taken seriously.

This chapter maps these content harms, first exploring the forms that harmful content can take in social VR environments and how VR renders these harms particularly acute. We then examine existing approaches to mitigating online content harms—community guidelines and human and automated content moderation—and their applicability for social VR.

Speech, Objects, Environments—Understanding Harmful Content in Social VR

The challenge of moderating harmful content in social VR largely mirrors the challenges encountered on 2D social media platforms. For instance, within existing social VR platforms, users can experience harmful speech such as harassment, racial abuse and homophobic slurs through text-based messaging, verbal comments,[6] imagery and other platform affordances.[7] Users may also be exposed to violent or sexually explicit content,[8] harmful ideologies, misinformation and propaganda.[9] The novel element for social VR platforms and their users is that the embodied nature of VR, synchronicity of interactions and perception of a shared physical space can all serve to create a more compelling experience with a more intense psychological impact,[10] when compared to similar exposure on 2D social media.[11]

On immersive platforms, objects and built environments can also be deployed to cause harm to users. A high-profile incident that played out on *Roblox*—a gaming platform that relies on user-generated scenarios and spaces—foreshadows how built environments can be used to cause harm. *Roblox* was found to be hosting recreations of the Christchurch mosque mass shooting in which a far-right extremist targeted New Zealand's Muslim community. During an extended period in 2021, using the search term 'Christchurch' on *Roblox* returned results containing multiple games that allowed users to re-enact the massacre. Whilst *Roblox* has not provided a full account of how these games passed its review process, it is likely that the keywords and user-generated environments for each game were only understood as clearly harmful when placed within their broader social context.

Community Guidelines—Fostering Pro-social Norms in Social VR

A 2022 study by researchers at UC Berkeley concluded that VR platforms should draw on existing social media community guidelines as a baseline for governing social VR.[12] These frameworks tend to be comprehensive—adapted and expanded by platforms over time in response to real-world issues—and so can serve as a valuable foundation for proactively prohibiting the types of harmful content that may arise in VR environments. This is important because research into gaming cultures and social media communities suggests that the absence of well-defined rules during the early stages of a platform's adoption can see norms emerge that are harmful to vulnerable and marginalised users.[13] By making use of existing governance regimes, social VR platforms can take early action to set clear expectations of their users in support of safe immersive spaces.

A valuable affordance of VR is that community guidelines can be displayed and engaged with by users in innovative ways to continually remind people of the principles of good behaviour. The VR platform *RecRoom*, for example, has summarised versions of its guidelines displayed next to entryways and in other communal locations. *RecRoom* also has a moderator-initiated warning system that aims to inform and educate new players when they may be at risk of breaching a guideline. *Horizon Worlds* similarly has a 'warnings' feature through which 'community guides' (Meta employees) can send pop-up messages to users warning of a potential rule violation; and if they wish to continue to participate in the space, the user must actively dismiss the warning.

Importantly, studies of social media show that when it comes to enforcing community guidelines, having punishments for rule violations does not properly deter rule-breaking—adherence to platform rules also requires a culture of compliance.[14] A 2023 study of content moderation rule-breaking on Facebook concluded that for matters associated with a high risk of causing harm—such as stalking, harassment, hate speech, financial scams and gun sales—culture-based governance interventions, in addition to punishments, are particularly important.[15] Justice scholars have argued, for instance, that requiring apologies from users who have harassed or abused others can work to ensure an offender takes responsibility for their actions and, at the same time, indicate that the platform condemns the harmful behaviour, both of which strengthen pro-social norms.[16] Advising users who are the victims of harmful behaviour of the outcome of complaints is also supportive of pro-social cultures. Fiani et al. (2023) explain that unclear outcomes can create the perception that there are no consequences for behaving badly, which can have the effect of encouraging antisocial behaviour.[17] This is why community guidelines should be understood as just an important first step towards creating safe VR environments—to be effective, guidelines must be enforced through a range of additional content moderation interventions that foster cultures of compliance.

Human, AI and Community Enforcement—A Multidimensional Approach to Content Moderation

A common feature of social VR is the ability for users to manipulate and create unique spaces for social and private play, communication and, in some cases, work. For the moderation of these spaces to be effective at preventing harm, a multidimensional approach is needed.

Automated moderation systems that utilise machine learning can be used to oversee online spaces for potential rule violations. This approach often involves the use of natural language processing (NLP) to automatically filter and block content containing specific terms, responding in real time to spoken words. An exemplary model of this application is the service *ToxMod*,[18] which monitors in-game voice chat on platforms such as *RecRoom*.[19] Using machine learning technology, *ToxMod* identifies, flags and reports instances of inappropriate behaviour to human moderators. Researchers have also demonstrated the potential for NLP to identify language patterns associated with bullies and their victims, automatically deleting offensive posts and comments.[20] However, in their research on AI-based moderation for handling harassment in social VR, Schulenberg et al. (2023) also caution that existing AI tools may struggle to differentiate genuine harassment from non-harassing content, such as the 'mock impoliteness' used by LGBTQ + communities to cope with hostility and abuse.[21] Another significant limitation of automated monitoring is that it tends to be ***reactive*** and cannot prevent harm in social VR environments where communication is synchronous.

Schulenberg et al. (2023) argue that to address the unique challenges of moderating synchronous interactions in social VR, moderation should follow a principle of ***user-human-AI collaboration***. This approach calls for contextually determined solutions rather than a one-size-fits-all strategy, where AI is one tool that human moderators can use to support content moderation decision-making. Human intervention is particularly important where VR content is created by users or third-party content providers and made available to the public, because automated systems are not good at understanding contextual nuances or the social or cultural significance of specific content to specific user groups—as indicated by the case of the Christchurch mosque re-enactments on *Roblox*.

Understanding the social and cultural context of user speech, objects and environments in social VR is also important for correctly identifying harmful content as user practices evolve over time. A large body of research into social media shows how users develop 'platform vernaculars'—novel ways of communicating that convey specific meanings on a particular platform.[22] Platform vernaculars can be harmless and playful, but they can also be used to evade content rules and moderation systems.[23] For example, pro-eating disorder communities have been shown to make substitutions for terms likely to trigger content moderation.[24] To convey hate, white nationalists often rely on 'dog whistling' to implicitly communicate hateful or inflammatory messages.[25] Humour is also commonly used to conceal or excuse hate speech and harassment.[26]

This type of implicitly harmful content can typically only be identified through a contextual interpretation undertaken by humans. In an interview for the *MIT Technology Review*, a content moderator for *Horizon Worlds* confirmed that moderation on the platform is highly complex and that to be able to make appropriate decisions, moderators must have a strong grasp of content guidelines and the ability to discern context.[27]

The use of human moderators in regulating social VR presents significant equity issues. Bias in content moderation is well documented. For instance, YouTube's content moderation, undertaken in large part by Filipino workforces, has been shown to mislabel Queer/LGBTQI + content as sexual in nature.[28] Other studies suggest that moderation often disproportionately impacts marginalised identities, such as Black and transgender users.[29] In this context, to curb biases and prevent undue restrictions on marginalised users' speech in social VR, it is important that moderation teams are diverse, well-trained and well-supported.

Adapting moderation practices for private, semi-public and public spaces is also important for safe and inclusive social VR. Users in public spaces—areas that are open to all platform users for exploration and social interactions—present the greatest risk of exposure to harmful content. Indicatively, Microsoft, the owner of *AltspaceVR*, discontinued its public spaces feature *Social Hubs* reportedly because the space was so difficult to moderate successfully. Public spaces require intensive moderation practices to successfully protect users from harm. In private VR spaces, on the other hand, where access is restricted to a select group of approved or invited users, community moderation has an important role to play. Empowering community actors—creators of a space and other trustworthy users—to moderate spaces comes with two significant advantages: it promotes the development of community-specific, pro-social norms and it eases the burden of administrating reports of inappropriate conduct by enabling community members to take actions at the time of an incident—by publicly condemning or ejecting a user from a space, for example.

For social VR spaces that house adult content (without breaching community guidelines)—such as stand-up comedy clubs, phobia exposure experiences or trauma support groups—content warnings can play an important role in keeping users safe. These warnings serve to inform users about the nature of the spaces they are about to enter, requiring explicit consent before granting access. Content warnings are particularly suitable for user-generated worlds in social VR and semi-public spaces, such as 'members-only' worlds, where the norms and social behaviours may vary and be locally specific. *RecRoom*, for instances, has a 'warning' feature that creators can use to advise other users about the content of the room, with default options including spooky/scary themes, mature themes, bright/flashing lights, intense motion, gore/violence, in addition to an option for a custom warning. These warnings appear when users try to join a *RecRoom* space. *Horizon Worlds* has a mature worlds policy (meaning 18+), requiring user-created worlds to be labelled mature if they contain sexually suggestive content, excessively violent content or are dedicated to drugs, alcohol and other age-regulated activities.[30] Charles et al. (2022) provide the Narrative Experiences Online (NEON) content-warning typology that can be utilised by social VR platforms for indicating what types of content should receive content warnings.[31] Content warning systems are especially useful when the content in a space does not break platform rules but may still be content certain users would prefer to avoid due to personal preference—those users can make informed decisions about their own comfort and safety.

Content Harms in a Mixed Reality Future

VR intensifies the psychological impact of harmful content. As we have discussed, this can include heightening the distress caused by exposure to violent, graphic or otherwise disturbing content, and enhancing the impact of false or misleading information, harmful ideologies and propaganda. In this chapter, we have explored present approaches deployed to help prevent these types of content harm, recognising the relative strengths and limitations. Ultimately, best practices will require a combination of context-aware human moderation, supported by AI, alongside interventions that foster cultures of compliance and pro-social norms.

The challenge of moderating virtual content is likely to increase in complexity as the XR industry introduces more augmented and mixed reality products. These systems allow users to interact with digital content overlaid across the physical world. As we have discussed in this chapter, we know from social VR that keeping public virtual spaces safe is particularly difficult. Futurist Mark Pesce reflects on how this might manifest in a more mixed reality future:

> What if that blank canvas gets painted with hate speech? What if, perchance, the homes of 'undesirables' are singled out with graffiti that

> only bad actors can see? What happens when every gathering place for any oppressed community gets invisibly 'tagged'? In short, what happens when bad actors use Facebook's augmented reality to amplify their own capacity to act badly?[32]

This future is not theoretical: *Mark AR*, for instance, is a mobile application that allows the creation and placement of persistent digital images in real-world environments.[33] With the release of the Apple Vision Pro in February 2024, early adopters have been seen with headsets adorned whilst driving, taking public transport and walking through crowded urban areas (using, for example, augmented maps viewed through the headset's outward facing cameras). Where Google Glass failed, perhaps Apple's device will represent the moment in which XR penetrates everyday life. Moderating this type of technology early and comprehensively will be key for minimising harm within and without of immersive spaces.

Notes

1. Baker-White, E. "Meta Wouldn't Tell Us How It Enforces Its Rules In VR, So We Ran a Test to Find Out." *BuzzFeed News*, February 12, 2022. https://www.buzzfeednews.com/article/emilybakerwhite/meta-facebook-horizon-vr-content-rules-test.
2. Amarasingam, A., and Marc-André, A. "The QAnon Conspiracy Theory: A Security Threat in the Making." *CTC Sentinel* 13, No. 7 (2020): 37–44.
3. Meta, Inc. "An Update to How We Address Movements and Organizations Tied to Violence." August 19, 2020. https://about.fb.com/news/2020/08/addressing-movements-and-organizations-tied-to-violence/.
4. Marwick, A., and Partin, W. "Constructing Alternative Facts: Populist Expertise and the QAnon Conspiracy." *New Media & Society* (2022).
5. United Nations Office of Counter-Terrorism. "Safeguarding the Metaverse: Countering Terrorism and Preventing Violent Extremism in Digital Space–Expert Panel." *United Nations Office of Counter-Terrorism*, November 28, 2022. https://www.un.org/counterterrorism/events/safeguarding-metaverse-countering-terrorism-and-preventing-violent-extremism-digital-space.

6. We classify verbal speech as a form of content because it is machine readable, and thus presents similar governance challenges to 'static' content. However, its synchronicity and ephemerality in VR mean it also shares many of the challenges associated with moderating conduct in VR.
7. Outlaw, J. "Harassment in Social VR: Stories from Survey Respondents." *Medium*, May 9, 2018. https://jessica-outlaw.medium.com/harassment-in-social-vr-stories-from-survey-respondents-59c9cde7ac02.
8. Zheng, Q., Xu, S., Wang, L., Tang, Y., Salvi, R., Freeman, G., and Huang, Y. "Understanding Safety Risks and Safety Design in Social VR Environments." *Proceedings of the ACM on Human-Computer Interaction* 7(CSCW1): 1–37.
9. Madiega, T., Car, P., Niestadt, M., and van der Pol, L. "Metaverse: Opportunities, Risks and Policy Implications." *European Parliament Research Service*, June 2022. https://www.europarl.europa.eu/RegData/etudes/BRIE/2022/733557/EPRS_BRI(2022)733557_EN.pdf.
10. Blackwell, L., Ellison, N., Elliott-Deflo, N., and Schwartz, R. "Harassment in Social Virtual Reality: Challenges for Platform Governance." In *Proceedings of the 2019 CHI Conference on Human-Computer Interaction*. USA (2019): 1–25.
11. Madiega, T., Car, P., Niestadt, M., and van der Pol, L. "Metaverse: Opportunities, Risks and Policy Implications." *European Parliament Research Service*, June 2022. https://www.europarl.europa.eu/RegData/etudes/BRIE/2022/733557/EPRS_BRI(2022)733557_EN.pdf.
12. Lazerson, R. "A Secure and Equitable Metaverse Designing Effective Community Guidelines for Social VR." *Centre for Long-Term Cybersecurity UC Berkeley*, November 2022. https://cltc.berkeley.edu/wp-content/uploads/2022/11/Secure_Equitable_Metaverse.pdf.
13. Massanari, A. "# Gamergate and The Fappening: How Reddit's Algorithm, Governance, and Culture Support Toxic Technocultures." *New Media & Society* 19, No. 3 (2017): 329–346.
14. Gillett, R., Gray, J., and Kaye, D. B. V. "'Just a Little Hack': Investigating Cultures of Content Moderation Circumvention by Facebook Users." *New Media & Society* (2023).
15. Ibid.

16. Schoenebeck, S., Haimson, O., and Nakamura, L. "Drawing from Justice Theories to Support Targets of Online Harassment." *New Media & Society* 23, No. 5 (2021): 1278–1300.
17. Fiani, C., Bretin, R., Mcgill, M., and Khamis, M. "Big Buddy: Exploring Child Reactions and Parental Perceptions Towards a Simulated Embodied Moderating System for Social Virtual Reality." In *Proceedings of the 22nd Annual ACM Interaction Design and Children Conference*. Chicago, USA (2023): 1–13.
18. Modulate. "Toxicity Moderation AI." July 15, 2023. https://www.modulate.ai/tox-mod.
19. Kou, Y., and Gui, X. "Flag and Flaggability in Automated Moderation: The Case of Reporting Toxic Behavior in an Online Game Community." *Proceedings of the 2021 CHI Conference on Human Factors in Computing Systems*: 1–12; Stoop, W., Kunneman, F., van den Bosch, A., and Miller, B. "Detecting Harassment in Real-Time as Conversations Develop." *Proceedings of the Third Workshop on Abusive Language Online* (2021): 19–24.
20. Basu, P., Singha Roy, T., Tiwari, S., and Mehta, S. "CyberPolice: Classification of Cyber Sexual Harassment." In *EPIA Conference on Artificial Intelligence* (2021): 701–714; Reynolds, K., Kontostathis, A., and Edwards, L. "Using Machine Learning to Detect Cyberbullying." In *2011 10th International Conference on Machine Learning and Applications and Workshops* (2011): 241–244.
21. Schulenberg, K., Li, L., Freeman, G., Zamanifard, S., and McNeese, N. "Towards Leveraging AI-Based Moderation to Address Emergent Harassment in Social Virtual Reality." In *Proceedings of the 2023 CHI Conference on Human Factors in Computing Systems*. Hamburg, Germany (2023): 1–17.
22. Gibbs, M., Meese, J., Arnold, M., Nansen, B., and Carter, M. "# Funeral and Instagram: Death, Social Media, and Platform Vernacular." *Information, Communication and Society* 18, No. 3 (2015): 255–268.
23. Gillett, R., Gray, J., and Kaye, D. B. V. "'Just a Little Hack': Investigating Cultures of Content Moderation Circumvention by Facebook Users." *New Media & Society* (2023).
24. Gerrard, Y. "Beyond the Hashtag: Circumventing Content Moderation on Social Media." *New Media & Society* 20, No. 12 (2018): 4492–4511.

25. Bhat, P., and Klein, O. "Covert Hate Speech: White Nationalists and Dog Whistle Communication on Twitter." In *Twitter, the Public Sphere, and the Chaos of Online Deliberation*, ed. Gwen Bouvier and Judith E. Rosenbaum (Cham: Springer, 2020): 151–172; Gillett, R., Gray, J., and Kaye, D. B. V. "'Just a Little Hack': Investigating Cultures of Content Moderation Circumvention by Facebook Users." *New Media & Society* (2023).
26. Siapera, E., and Viejo-Otero, P. "Governing Hate: Facebook and Digital Racism." *Television & New Media* 22, No. 2 (2021): 112–130.
27. Ryan-Mosely, T. "How an Undercover Content Moderator Polices the Metaverse." *MIT Technology Review*, April 28, 2023.
28. Romano, A. "YouTubers Claim the Site Systematically Demonetizes LGBTQ Content." *Vox*, October 10, 2019. https://www.vox.com/culture/2019/10/10/20893258/youtube-lgbtq-censorship-demonetization-nerd-city-algorithm-report.
29. Haimson, O. L., Delmonaco, D., Nie, P., and Wegner, A. "Disproportionate Removals and Differing Content Moderation Experiences for Conservative, Transgender, and Black Social Media Users: Marginalization and Moderation Gray Areas." *Proceedings of the ACM on Human-Computer Interaction* 5(CSCW2) (2021): 1–35.
30. Meta. "Meta Horizon Worlds Mature and Prohibited Worlds Policy." *Meta Quest Help*, November 2022. https://www.meta.com/en-gb/help/quest/articles/horizon/create-in-horizon-worlds/restrictions-to-worlds-in-horizon/.
31. See Charles, A., Hare-Duke, L., Nudds, H., Franklin, D., Llewellyn-Beardsley, J., Rennick-Egglestone, S., ... Slade, M. "Typology of Content Warnings and Trigger Warnings: Systematic Review." *PloS One* 17, No. 5 (2022): e0266722.
32. Pesce, M. *Augmented Reality: Unboding Tech's Next Big Thing*. New Jersey, USA: Wiley, 2020.
33. Robertson, A. "Is the World Ready for Virtual Graffiti?" *The Verge*, October 13, 2019. https://www.theverge.com/2019/10/12/20908824/mark-ar-google-cloud-anchors-social-art-platform-harassment-moderation.

CHAPTER 3

Conduct Harms in Social VR: Embodied Harassment, Gender-Based Harm and Toxic Cultures

Abstract This chapter delves into the complexities of conduct harms in social Virtual Reality (VR), emphasising the distinctive challenges posed by VR's immersive nature. It explores how VR's spatial and temporal affordances intensify experiences of harassment, particularly embodied harassment, which feels 'real' due to the embodied nature of VR interactions. The chapter highlights the inadequacy of current moderation practices and the unique forms of gender-based harm prevalent within VR environments. It critiques the reliance on reactive safety features, which often fail to protect users effectively, and underscores the necessity for a more proactive approach to governance and policymaking. By examining the psychological and social impacts of conduct harms, the chapter calls for a reevaluation of community norms and the development of more inclusive and effective moderation tools, advocating for a synergy between human, automated and community-based approaches to ensure user safety in social VR platforms.

Keywords Virtual reality · Conduct harms · Embodied harassment · VR harassment · Social virtual reality · Moderation practices · Gender-based harm · Toxic cultures · Online communities · Safety feature abuse

J. E. Gray et al., *Governing Social Virtual Reality*,
https://doi.org/10.1007/978-3-031-61831-4_3

Introduction

Social VR introduces a paradigm shift in digital communication by combining the immediacy of both verbal and nonverbal interactions, with a strong sense of presence and embodiment within a virtual space. This experience, fundamentally different from traditional 'flat-screen' media such as film and television, is crafted through natural user interfaces including voice, gaze and body-tracking, facilitating a sense of being truly 'in place'. The spatial and temporal dimensions of VR—where users are represented by avatars and interactions are both ephemeral and synchronous—present unique platform governance challenges, including the moderation of user *conduct*. Effective governance of conduct in social VR must account for VR's inherent technological affordances of temporality and spatiality, which shape user behaviours in ways that are distinct from other forms of media. In this chapter, we explain how the affordances of VR can amplify embodied harassment (including gender-based harassment) and we examine the limitations of current approaches to user safety in social VR.

Embodied Harassment—VR Feels 'Very Real'

Immersive conduct shapes many of the positive experiences associated with VR—such as the ability to feel more intimately connected to other users, or the ability to create high-fidelity simulations where the user feels physically present. Yet, these same affordances also have the potential to bring about significant user harm. For instance, a player of the VR game *Hover Junkers* reported feeling unusually disturbed after witnessing another player's in-game suicide. They explained that the player's movements and body language made the experience feel 'real'.[1]

Presence and avatar movement can also cause discomfort, distress or harm in instances such as unwanted touching, standing too close to another avatar, obstructing movement or performing visibly sexual gestures—constituting what is known as *embodied harassment*.[2] Embodiment in VR describes how personal space and interpersonal boundaries, taken for granted in the physical world, are perceptually carried over into VR—along with the distress felt when these boundaries are breached.[3] Embodied harassment is not equivalent to physical, real-world harassment, but it is distinct from the verbal harassment that occurs in 2D social media. Indeed, people subject to harassment in social VR have reported being surprised at how real it feels, despite knowing it is only virtual. Importantly, in social VR, harassment does not have to involve physical acts such as groping or touching. Studies indicate that the act of approaching another user too closely in VR can trigger discomfort and violate norms of personal distance.[4] Empirical work has demonstrated the relationship between proxemics (of human avatars and objects) and physiological response in virtual environments.[5] In contrast to flat-screen media where proximity is not personally intrusive, the immersive nature of VR means that even non-contact interactions can be perceived as invasive, due to the visceral connection users feel between their physical selves and their avatars.

The potential for harassment is especially high in social VR applications that focus on general social interactions between users, rather than on a shared activities such as playing games or watching a concert or sporting event. Generalist social VR applications, where there is no structured activity, often facilitate interactions between strangers, partly because of VR's synchronous nature—your friends may not be online when you are—and its relatively low adoption rate—your friends may not own a VR headset. Harassment in this type of VR setting was vividly illustrated by VR researcher Nina Jane Patel who was "verbally and sexually harassed" within the first minute of joining Meta's *Oculus Venues*. Patel described how it "was a horrible experience that happened so fast, and before I could even think about activating the safety barrier. I froze".[6] The incident underscores how VR's synchronous affordances—combined with the tendency for users to interact with strangers—expose people to the risk of harmful social interactions.

There is consensus across academic work that embodied harassment needs to be taken seriously as a form of harassment and/or assault. Katherine Cross—a scholar studying online harassment—argues that "the mediating interface of a game does not make abusive behaviour between two or more real people any less abusive. Slurs are still slurs; unwanted sexual advances are still both unwanted and sexual".[7] Legal scholar John Danaher similarly argues that some instances of what he terms 'virtual sexual assault' are real, "because virtual sexual assault can have real world consequences", that is to say, real harm, "and there are some grounds for thinking that certain aspects of sexual activity are social, as opposed to physical, in nature".[8]

The significance of embodied harassment has been acknowledged by certain social VR platforms in their platform policies. For instance,

AltSpaceVR—a social VR platform that was purchased and eventually closed by Microsoft—explained in its Community Standards that:

> AltspaceVR offers a truly unique environment where verbal communication and non-verbal gestures and spatial positioning can lead to a rich user experience. However, this also means that users might experience social discomfort if their personal space is violated in ways that would be deemed inappropriate in real life. Continuing such behaviour after a user has expressed discomfort constitutes harassment and can lead to account suspension or termination.

AltspaceVR's position is supported by research that has found that embodiment in VR can amplify the consequences of harmful conduct.[9] For instance, participants in a study by Zheng et al. (2023) reported that aggressive behaviour in VR, such as a physical attack by another avatar, produced a phantom pain sensation, the brain seemingly perceiving virtual harm as a physical phenomenon.[10] Virtual harm has begun to draw the attention of lawmakers—for example, a European Parliament report on 'the metaverse' noted that harmful VR content can feel very 'real' and 'violating'.[11] Media reportage on social VR platforms has also focused heavily on the pervasiveness of embodied harassment, and its serious and harmful effects.[12]

Addressing the issue of embodied harassment is most pressing for marginalised groups, including women and racial minorities, who are at a higher risk of experiencing online harms. Alarmingly, user responses to VR harassment often downplay its significance and place the onus on the victim to end the experience, suggesting, for example, that a female user "could easily turn off, or just take off her headset to escape".[13] This sentiment echoes the ways in which violence against women has been downplayed historically,[14] and is unacceptable because it excludes women from safely participating in social VR spaces, perpetuating a problem that has pervaded social media and gaming platforms for decades.

Gender-Based Harm—A Pervasive Problem

One of the most prominent early pieces of writing about VR harassment was by UX researcher and author Jordan Belamire, who documented her experience of sexual assault in the form of 'virtual groping' that occurred when she played the social VR archery game *QuiVr*. All *QuiVr* avatars look the same; a Viking helmet, no body and two floating hands. In between shooting at waves of zombies, a player on Belamire's team moved over to where she was standing in the game and 'suddenly', she described, his "disembodied helmet faced me dead-on. His floating hand approached my body, and he started to virtually rub my chest". Despite yelling stop and trying to get away "he chased me around, making grabbing and pinching motions near my chest. Emboldened, he even shoved his hand toward my virtual crotch and began rubbing".[15]

Outside of the immersion of VR, Belamire concedes that the interaction might have looked 'pretty funny', and not real. But, as we have discussed, because VR affords the user an immersive, haptically, auditorily and visually rich experience, our bodies can respond to conduct as if it were real. This is why VR can be used to treat animal phobias—a VR-encounter with a spider provokes the same psycho-social response as a real-life encounter, for instance.[16] In describing her sexual assault in VR, Belamire explains, "the virtual groping feels just as real. Of course, you're not physically being touched ... but it's still scary as hell". To accept the positive potential VR—that provides a profound immersive experience—means we must also accept its negative potential.

Other forms of gender-based harassment that have been described by social VR users include 'creepy' behaviour, such as silent staring and taking photographs; groping, such as by simulating unwanted touching; stalking, by following despite objections; simulated sex acts, such as using hands or virtual objects to mimic penetration; rape threats and jokes, such as about 'force feeding' women alcohol; and situations described as a 'gang rape'. Troublingly, research suggests that these experiences are commonplace for women in social VR. A 2018 survey of VR users found that 49% of women respondents and 36% of male respondents had experienced sexual harassment in VR.[17] A 2019 study, conducted by Oculus, found 22% of users reported having 'uncomfortable' experiences in social VR.[18] A 2023 study by the Centre for Countering Digital Hate found that in 20% of Horizon World environments, users encountered sexually explicit harassment, racist abuse and misogyny within five minutes of joining the space.[19]

In an experience similar to the one described by Nina Jane Patel, non-profit advocacy group *SumOfUs* reported that a researcher from their organisation was in *Horizon Worlds* for less than an hour before she experienced sexual assault. Without consent, a user simulated sex with her avatar, whilst another user watched and drank a bottle of vodka, eventually offering her the bottle and saying, "here you're going to need more of this".[20] Media investigations into *Horizon Worlds* and other social VR platforms such as *VRChat* have routinely uncovered similar behaviours, including instances where child users have been subjected to rape jokes and sexually explicit threats.[21]

The prevalence of gender-based harassment in VR can be attributed to VR's basis in masculinised 'gamer' culture.[22] As scholars have observed, proudly "designed for gamers, by gamers", the original Oculus Kickstarter catered specifically to the core values of hardcore gamer culture "without addressing associated issues surrounding gender and misogyny".[23] Toxicity in gamer culture is typically attributed to marketing through the 1990s that emphasised hypermasculinity (competitiveness and violence) alongside hyper-sexual and misogynistic advertisements.[24] Whilst behaviours like 'griefing' and 'trolling' have an extensive history in online games, academics who study game communities argue that targeted harassment is a form of gatekeeping in line with an adherence to hypermasculinity.[25] Players who ignore insults "demonstrate a cool-headed rationality...traditionally associated with the performance of masculinity".[26] Meanwhile, 'reacting' exhibits 'feminine' and 'emotional' traits. This worldview incentivises players to engage in toxic behaviours to establish membership in the community and avoid becoming targets themselves. Harassment campaigns like 'GamerGate'[27] fit within this understanding; they are instances of 'boundary work' that seek to establish what kinds of behaviours, values and players are acceptable (e.g., masculine, competitive, right-wing, male) and what are not (e.g., feminine, cooperative, inclusive). By explicitly soliciting the hardcore gamer community as early adopters of VR without addressing its known cultural problems, Meta, Valve and other early VR developers have effectively fostered a misogynist VR culture.[28]

Clashing social norms about how people should behave in online spaces also contributes to gender-based harassment, including the plausible deniability of play.[29] Again, this is due in part to the social norms transferred from gaming to social VR. For instance, in gamer culture, 'tea bagging'—the act of crouching repeatedly over another player's body after the player has been killed—is commonplace, to the extent that many games have designed-in the ability for tea bagging. VR users, encultured in gaming communities, may see this type of avatar-to-avatar interaction as an appropriate way to interact in social VR despite it constituting a form of embodied sexual harassment.[30] As Schulenberg et al. (2023) note, this is one of the primary challenges for mitigating harassment in social VR: a "lack of consensus amongst social VR users on what social norms/behaviours are harassing rather than simply inappropriate or 'fun/play' creates barriers to effectively define and identify harassment, as a diverse array of individuals and communities may have different understandings".[31]

User-Centric Safety Features—Misuse and Abuse

Nick Clegg, Meta's President of Global Affairs, has argued that conduct moderation in social VR should be driven by the user. Clegg thinks that we should consider conduct in virtual spaces as analogous to conduct in a real-world environment such as a bar.[32] He explains,

> in the US, we wouldn't hold a bar manager responsible for real-time speech moderation in their bar, as if they should stand over your table, listen intently to your conversation, and silence you if they hear things they don't like... we would expect them to use their discretion to exclude disruptive customers who don't respond to reasonable warnings about their behaviour. And we would expect customers who were upset by aggressive or inappropriate speech to be able to speak to the manager about it, and for some kind of action to result

Thus, according to Clegg, in social VR, the onus for moderating harm should primarily be on the VR user—the bar patron. Consistent with this view, Meta has generally responded to reports of conduct harms on its platform by suggesting that users should better utilise the platform's safety features, especially the personal boundary, a setting that results in virtual hands and avatars disappearing when a user enters another user's personal space.[33]

Placing the responsibility for managing harmful conduct on to users is at odds with research showing that safety tools do not always work as intended and are subject to misuse. An illustrative example was reported in *New York* magazine regarding the Soapstone stand-up comedy club space in Meta's *Horizon Worlds*.[34] Journalist Paul Murray reported that he witnessed harassment during a stand-up performance. A user named Texasmarshall directed insults at performers and then targeted another user who entered the space, RicardoCortazar. Texasmarshall hurled racist and derogatory remarks at RicardoCortazar, including saying "he's a good little Mexican boy. He's gonna check my tires for me later".

RicardoCortazar responded to the abuse by saying, "Why are you saying this to me? Is it because I'm colored?" Texasmarshall then reported RicardoCortazar for using the term 'colored', and the crowd voted RicardoCortazar out of the club using *Horizon Worlds'* poll-to-remove feature, through which users can vote to evict another user from a space. Ironically, a tool designed to empower users to address bad behaviour was in this instance used to silence a victim of abuse. When Murray, the journalist who had been observing the scene, questioned the fairness of these actions, he too was ejected via the poll-to-remove feature. The incident demonstrates how user-centric safety mechanisms—comparable to real-world examples such when the 'find my phone' feature has been exploited for stalking or coercive control—can be weaponised to harm others, a practice that is well documented in social media research.[35]

As discussed in Chapter 2, pro-social norms are needed for safe online spaces. A user-centred approach to conduct moderation unfairly shifts the burden of combating bad behaviour on to victims who are often women and other marginalised users and fails to address deeper issues within toxic online cultures. It is also increasingly at odds with a global legislative trend towards requiring platforms to take an active role in preventing user harm (discussed further in Chapter 7), in recognition of the role these platforms play in creating environments that facilitate such harms.[36]

In this chapter, we have argued that the unique spatial and temporal affordances of VR can facilitate profound experiences of connection, sociality and presence. Yet, like any technology, VR is Janus faced. It also has the potential to materialise harm. Effectively moderating user conduct in social VR, as is the case with moderating content, is likely to depend on a synergy between human, automated and community-based interventions.

Notes

1. Buckley, S. "I Watched Someone Commit Suicide in VR and It Freaked Me Out." *Engadget*, January 28, 2016. https://www.engadget.com/2016-01-28-i-watched-someone-commit-suicide-in-vr-and-it-freaked-me-out.html.
2. Schulenberg, K., Li, L., Freeman, G., Zamanifard, S., and McNeese, N. J. "Towards Leveraging AI-Based Moderation to

Address Emergent Harassment in Social Virtual Reality." In *Proceedings of the 2023 CHI Conference on Human Factors in Computing Systems* (2023, April): 1–17.

3. See Murphy, D. J. "Virtual Reality Is 'Finally Here': A Qualitative Exploration of Formal Determinants of Player Experience in VR." In *DiGRA Conference* (2017, July); Llobera, J., Spanlang, B., Ruffini, G., and Slater, M. "Proxemics with Multiple Dynamic Characters in an Immersive Virtual Environment." *ACM Transactions on Applied Perception (TAP)* 8, No. 1 (2010): 1–12.
4. Freeman, G., Zamanifard, S., Maloney, D., and Acena, D. "Disturbing the Peace: Experiencing and Mitigating Emerging Harassment in Social Virtual Reality." *Proceedings of the ACM on Human-Computer Interaction* 6(CSCW1) (2022): 1–30.
5. Ibid.
6. Patel, N. "Reality or Fiction?" *Medium*, December 22, 2021. https://medium.com/kabuni/fiction-vs-non-fiction-98aa0098f3b0.
7. Cross, K. "Online Harm Is real." *Slate*, November 14, 2016. https://slate.com/technology/2016/11/sexual-harassment-in-virtual-reality-is-real.html.
8. Danaher, J. "The Law and Ethics of Virtual Sexual Assault." In *The Law of Virtual and Augmented Reality*, ed. Marc Blitz and Woodrow Barfield (Cheltenham, UK: Edward Elgar Press, 2018).
9. Blackwell, L., Ellison, N., Elliott-Deflo, N., and Schwartz, R. "Harassment in Social Virtual Reality: Challenges for Platform Governance." *Proceedings of the ACM on Human-Computer Interaction* 3(CSCW) (2019): 1–25.
10. Zheng, Q., Xu, S., Wang, L., Tang, Y., Salvi, R. C., Freeman, G., and Huang, Y. "Understanding Safety Risks and Safety Design in Social VR Environments." *Proceedings of the ACM on Human-Computer Interaction* 7(CSCW1) (2023): 1–37.
11. Polona, C. A. R., André, M. T., and Maria, N. "Metaverse: Opportunities, Risks and Policy Implications," 2022. https://www.europarl.europa.eu/RegData/etudes/BRIE/2022/733557/EPRS_BRI(2022)733557_EN.pdf.
12. For instance, see Basu, T. "The Metaverse Has a Groping Problem Already." *MIT Technology Review*, December 16, 2021; Crawford, A., and Smith, T. "Metaverse App Allows Kids into Virtual Strip

Clubs." *BBC News*, February 22, 2022. https://www.bbc.com/news/technology-60415317; Bokinni, Y. "A Barrage of Assault, Racism and Rape Jokes: My Nightmare Trip into the Metaverse." *The Guardian*, April 25, 2022. https://www.theguardian.com/tv-and-radio/2022/apr/25/a-barrage-of-assault-racism-and-jokes-my-nightmare-trip-into-the-metaverse.

13. Sparrow, L. A., Antonellos, M., Gibbs, M., and Arnold, M. "From 'Silly' to 'Scumbag': Reddit Discussion of a Case of Groping in a Virtual Reality Game." In *Proceedings of the 2020 DiGRA International Conference: Play Everywhere, The Digital Games Research Association* (2020).
14. Hartnell, L. "It's Never Her Fault: End the Victim-Blaming." ABC News, April 1, 2016. https://www.abc.net.au/news/2016-04-01/victim-blaming-never-her-fault/7288468.
15. Belamire, J. "My First Virtual Reality Groping." *Athena Talks*, October 21, 2016. https://medium.com/athena-talks/my-first-virtual-reality-sexual-assault-2330410b62ee.
16. Powers, M. B., and Emmelkamp, P. M. "Virtual Reality Exposure Therapy for Anxiety Disorders: A Meta-Analysis." *Journal of Anxiety Disorders* 22, No. 3 (2008): 561–569.
17. "The Extended Mind". 2018. "Virtual Harassment: The Social Experience of 600 + Regular Virtual Reality Users." Slidedeck. https://drive.google.com/file/d/1afFQJN6QAwmeZdGcRj9R4ohVr0oZNO4a/view.
18. Blackwell, L., Ellison, N., Elliott-Deflo,. N., and Schwartz, R. "Harassment in Social Virtual Reality." In *Proceedings of the 2019 CHI Conference on Human-Computer Interaction* (2019): 1–25.
19. Centre for Countering Digital Hate. "Horizon Worlds Exposed." *CCDH Report*, March 2023. https://counterhate.com/research/horizon-worlds-exposed/.
20. SumOfUs. "Metaverse: Another Cesspool of Toxic Content," May 2022. https://www.eko.org/images/Metaverse_report_May_2022.pdf.
21. Crawford, A., and Smith, T. "Metaverse App Allows Kids into Virtual Strip Clubs." *BBC News*, February 22, 2022. https://www.bbc.com/news/technology-60415317; Bokinni, Y. "A Barrage of Assault, Racism and Rape Jokes: My Nightmare Trip

into the Metaverse." *The Guardian*, April 25, 2022. https://www.theguardian.com/tv-and-radio/2022/apr/25/a-barrage-of-assault-racism-and-jokes-my-nightmare-trip-into-the-metaverse.

22. Carter, M., and Egliston, B. *Fantasies of Virtual Reality* (MIT Press, 2024).
23. Foxman, M. "Making the Virtual a Reality: Playful Work and Playbour in the Diffusion of Innovations." *Digital Culture & Society* 7, No. 1 (2021): 91–110.
24. Kocurek, C. A. *Coin-Operated Americans: Rebooting Boyhood at the Video Game Arcade*. University of Minnesota Press, 2015. See also Jess Morrissette, "How Games Marketing Invented Toxic Gamer Culture." *VICE*, March 2020. https://www.vice.com/en/article/5dmayn/games-marketing-toxic-gamer-culture-online-xbox-live-dreamcast.
25. Bergstrom, K. "Destruction as Deviant Leisure in EVE Online." *Journal for Virtual Worlds Research* 13, No. 1 (2020).
26. Condis, M. *Gaming Masculinity: Trolls, Fake Geeks, and the Gendered Battle for Online Culture*. University of Iowa Press, 2018.
27. GamerGate was (and is) an internet-based harassment campaign against diverse players and game developers which commenced in 2014. See Gray, K. L. "Solidarity Is for White Women in Gaming." *Diversifying Barbie and Mortal Kombat: Intersectional Perspectives and Inclusive Designs in Gaming* (2016): 59–70; Chess, S., and Shaw, A. "A Conspiracy of Fishes, or, How We Learned to Stop Worrying About# GamerGate and Embrace Hegemonic Masculinity." *Journal of Broadcasting & Electronic Media* 59, No. 1 (2015): 208–220; Golding, D., and Van Deventer, L. *Game Changers*. Hachette UK, 2016.
28. As a further example, we'd be remiss here not to mention *Dead or Alive Xtreme 3*—a VR game available for the PlayStation 4—which allows players to grope the game's bikini clad non-player characters while she grimaces, protects her body with her arms, and says "I don't like it". In the video demo shared online that precipitated media attention, the male-sounding audience laughs in response. As legal scholar Mary Franks writes "the primary concern with games like these is not the harm one user inflicts on another actual user in a virtual reality environment, but the harmful habits the technology encourages the user to indulge."

See Franks, M. A. "The Desert of the Unreal: Inequality in Virtual and Augmented Reality." *UCDL Review* 51 (2017): 499. Writing in *Engadget*, Sean Buckley describes Dead or Alive Xtreme 3 as "sexual assault, the game". See Buckley, S. "I Watched Someone Commit Suicide in VR and It Freaked Me Out." Engadget, January 28, 2016. https://www.engadget.com/2016-01-28-i-watched-someone-commit-suicide-in-vr-and-it-freaked-me-out.html.

29. VRChat's community guidelines explicitly note that ""Role-playing" is not an excuse for violating the community guidelines.".
30. For instance, in 2016, games YouTuber PewDiePie (who was for several years the most subscribed to non-brand channel on YouTube) released an eight-part video series reviewing the HTC Vive. The first of these is simply titled, 'TEABAGGING IN VR'.
31. Schulenberg, K., Li, L., Freeman, G., Zamanifard, S., and McNeese, N. J. "Towards Leveraging AI-Based Moderation to Address Emergent Harassment in Social Virtual Reality." In *Proceedings of the 2023 CHI Conference on Human Factors in Computing Systems* (2023, April): 1–17.
32. Clegg, N. "Making the Metaverse: What It Is, How It Will Be Built, and Why It Matters." *Medium*, May 18, 2022. https://nickclegg.medium.com/making-the-metaverse-what-it-is-how-it-will-be-built-and-why-it-matters-3710f7570b04
33. Heath, A. "Meta Opens Up Access to Its VR Social Platform Horizon Worlds." *The Verge*. December 10, 2021. https://www.theverge.com/2021/12/9/22825139/meta-horizon-worlds-access-open-metaverse.
34. Murray, P. "Who Is Still Inside the Metaverse? Searching for Friends in Mark Zuckerberg's Deserted Fantasyland." *NYMag*, March 15, 2023, https://nymag.com/intelligencer/article/mark-zuckerberg-metaverse-meta-horizon-worlds.html
35. See, e.g., Are, C. "The Assemblages of Flagging and De-platforming Against Marginalised Content Creators." *Convergence*, 2023; Kaye, D. B. V., and Gray, J. E. "Copyright Gossip: Exploring Copyright Opinions, Theories, and Strategies on YouTube." *Social Media + Society* 7, No. 3 (2021).
36. Price, L. "Platform Responsibility for Online Harms: Towards a Duty of Care for Online Hazards." *Journal of Media Law* 13, No. 2 (2021): 238–261.

CHAPTER 4

Children and Social VR: Physiological, Psychological and Social Harms

Abstract This chapter explores the multifaceted impacts of social Virtual Reality (VR) on children, focusing on physiological, psychological and social harms. It highlights how the immersive nature of VR exacerbates concerns about children's digital media use, particularly when children are still developing important cognitive, social and physical skills. The chapter reviews research on the physiological effects of VR on children's vision and balance, discusses psychological concerns including the potential for addiction and the difficulty in distinguishing VR from reality and delves into social harms such as targeted harassment and exposure to mature content. The chapter emphasises the need for robust age-appropriate design, supervision and content moderation to protect young users in VR environments. It also addresses the broader implications of children's presence in social VR spaces for adult users, emphasising the need for community norms that support a safe and inclusive environment for all ages. Taken together, this overview adds to calls against the further expansion of children's use of VR without further research and safeguards.

Keywords Virtual reality · Children in VR · Physiological harms · Psychological impacts · Social harassment · Content moderation · Embodied harassment · Children online

J. E. Gray et al., *Governing Social Virtual Reality*,
https://doi.org/10.1007/978-3-031-61831-4_4

Introduction

When it comes to people under the age of 18 using social VR, many of the harms detailed so far in this book become more acute, and new harms emerge. This is largely due to the fact that children are still developing important cognitive skills and the immersive nature of VR can isolate young users from their social and safety networks. In this chapter, we review the potential harms to children in social VR, including physiological, psychological and social issues. Physiological harms primarily relate to issues of eye health and motion sickness. Psychological issues encompass children's abilities to distinguish VR from real life and the potential for addiction. Social issues include the potential for harassment, bullying and manipulation and the risk of exposure to mature content and conduct. Whilst platform safety features—for example, age-gating content—can go some way towards protecting young VR users, children remain a highly vulnerable user group within social VR and more research is needed to properly understand and combat these risks.

Physiological Harms—A Thirteen Plus Technology

Historically, the VR industry has opted to self-regulate as technology suitable only to users over the age of 13.[1] For example, when first launched, Meta's policy was that Quest headsets were only for users aged 13+ and they required third-party apps to ban users under the age of 13. This approach allowed the VR industry to avoid falling within the remit of the United States' 1998 *Children's Online Privacy Protection Act*, which applies to children 12 years old and under. It was also thought to be supported by research indicating that VR could negatively affect eye development in users under 13 years of age.[2]

Concerns about the impact of VR on the eye development of young users stem from studies conducted with early VR headset models which had drastically lower screen resolution than modern devices. The evidence regarding the impact of modern VR headsets is inconclusive. The results of a 2020 study challenged the notion that VR is unsafe for children aged 10 to 12 specifically, based on current ophthalmological findings.[3] As well, the *Children and Virtual Reality* project, undertaken by researchers at the University of Leeds, found no significant short-term effects on visual acuity in children.[4] However, the same study did find that for two out of the 20 young participants aged 8–12, there was a noted decrease in postural stability and stereoacuity, with one child experiencing worsened balance. Whilst such results may not be unique to children—since VR has also been shown to cause dizziness and temporary visual effects in adults—the study underscores the need for caution and further research into the physiological impacts of VR before it is made readily available to young children. In the meantime, time constraints and natural breaks during VR use should be used to minimise physiological harm to young (if not all) users.

Children are also at risk of experiencing motion sickness in VR, often referred to as VR sickness, which occurs when there's a disconnect between what the eyes see and what the body feels. For example, to simulate the experience of a roller coaster ride whilst the user is seated on a couch, a VR device will project a visual field that the eyes will perceive as movement. If the body is stationary (sitting on the couch), this visual information will clash with the sensory inputs from the inner ear's vestibular system, which detects balance and movement. These conflicting signals to the brain can result in symptoms associated with motion sickness—dizziness, nausea and disorientation.[5] This dissonance can be exacerbated for children using VR headsets that are designed for adults. Most headsets are calibrated for adult interpupillary distance (IPD)—the space between the pupils. IPD is typically narrower in children so they are more likely to experience a misalignment that can intensify the experience of VR sickness. As discussed further in Chapter 6, research by Kay Stanney et al. (2020) suggests that current approaches to VR headset design also contribute to a higher prevalence of VR sickness in women because VR headsets are typically designed with the average male IPD in mind.[6] Compared to adult male users, both women and children are at a higher risk of experiencing physical discomfort when using VR.

Psychological Harms—Cognitive Development and Impulse Control

Typically, two types of psychological harm are invoked in discussions about children and VR: their ability to distinguish VR from real life and the potential for addiction. Neither of these concerns are supported by research to the extent that they are sometimes portrayed in media. Instead, we argue, an evidence-based understanding of the potential for psychological harm amongst young VR users relates most directly to children's cognitive development and impulse control.

For example, research into experiences of VR amongst young users suggests that the ability of children to differentiate between VR and real-life experiences is a skill that develops with age. Claims that children are unable to make this distinction tend to be linked to a 2009 false-memory study which found that children aged four to five may confuse VR with mental imagery (imagining something), impacting their memory formation, but that this confusion appears to diminish with age, with no such effect observed in subjects six years and older.[7] A study by Liao et al. (2019), in which children aged six to eight were observed as they tested and assessed the 'reality' of VR—for example, by holding their breath when going under water—found that children understood the virtual space was not real, whilst still experiencing strong feelings of social presence and physiological and emotional responses to stimuli.[8] Overall, current research suggests that the ability to distinguish any type of media from reality is a learned skill that develops as children's cognitive skills advance and transform throughout various phases of childhood.[9]

Arguably, a more significant finding of Liao et al.'s (2019) study was that VR can isolate children "so that they are not getting cues from others in physical space that could help them process other media (e.g., seeing adult reactions to TV)".[10] Unlike TV or 2D games, where children often share experiences with adults and receive social cues, in social VR, children can miss out on important information that help in processing experiences. This is why researchers have argued that adult supervision is needed when children use VR.[11]

Questions about children and the potential for addiction to VR are often linked to broader debates about young people and video game addiction. To date, research specific to VR addiction is limited and even in gaming scholarship questions about addition are highly contested. Kiamara et al. (2022), in their examination of ethical considerations for VR use by children, concluded that it is unclear whether extensive gaming directly causes problematic behaviour or if those with impulse control disorders are naturally drawn to excessive gaming.[12] Our own research into gaming addiction similarly challenges classifications of addition that lack empirical support and may misrepresent children's gaming habits.[13] In our view, the real issue is not addiction; rather, it is that children are in the process of developing impulse control and this can lead to scenarios where they favour digital play over less stimulating activities or responsibilities such as homework or chores.[14] We suggest that social VR should be understood in this context—for young users who are still developing their impulse regulation, adult supervision, time limitations and built-in breaks during VR use will be critical for healthy practices.

Social Harms—Targeted Harassment, Manipulation and Mature Content

The potential for social harms in VR is particularly concerning for child users because they are typically more susceptible to harassment, bullying, manipulation, personal information disclosure and the negative effects of exposure to mature content. These online harms are well documented in social media research and have the potential to be amplified within the immersive environments of social VR.

As discussed in Chapters 2 and 3, in social VR, harassment can feel quite real. This is not to say that children cannot distinguish VR harassment from real harassment, but to acknowledge that VR can invoke psychological and emotional responses as if it were real. Several studies of social VR have uncovered significant harassment of child users. Researchers from the Centre for Countering Digital Hate identified instances of harassment towards young users in 20% of *Horizon Worlds* environments, including sexual and racial harassment. In their research, Maloney et al. (2020) similarly observed extensive derogatory comments towards minors in social VR, especially young girls.[15] They explain that due to voice chat, "children are particularly noticeable on social VR platforms", and are commonly subject to targeted harassment because of their age, for example, through the use of the denigratory term 'squeaker' (a reference to a lower pitched voice).[16] As Cristina Fiani et al. (2023) note, harassment in VR is highly problematic for children because most VR platforms do not facilitate remote parental oversight in the same way as 2D media, and it is generally difficult for parents to monitor what is going on within a headset.[17] For this reason, Common Sense Media has called for easier methods for casting VR to a mobile device so parents can monitor children's VR use.[18]

Parental oversight is also important because research suggests that children may be more susceptible to manipulation by other actors (human and AI) in social VR. Whilst children may know VR is not real, they have been shown to treat the characters they meet in VR as real social actors.[19] This aligns with research into other emerging technologies such as robot dogs and smart speakers which found that children have difficulty distinguishing between artificial social actors and real social actors, often viewing them as friendly, smart and trustworthy.[20] If children act with other social VR users in the same way they interact with people in real life—assuming they are trustworthy and that the interaction is safe—they will be vulnerable to grooming by adult users who can conceal their real age in social VR. These risks are further exacerbated in VR when the technology isolates children within a social environment that is difficult for parents to monitor.[21]

A final concern regarding children using social VR is the potential for exposure to mature content. The Centre for Countering Digital Hate identified several instances where minors accessed adult-oriented areas within *Horizon Worlds*, including venues themed around cannabis and explicit adult entertainment. In one instance, a human moderator, after a brief inquiry about age, permitted an underage user into an 18 + area, despite clear evidence from their Facebook profile indicating the user was underage.[22] This incident underscores the ease with which children can misrepresent their age in social VR potentially accessing and engaging with content and conversations unsuitable for their age group. The immersive nature of VR means that unintended encounters with adult content could have a more significant impact on young users (compared to 2D media) and if they are wearing an immersive device, it can be difficult for a child to quickly avert their gaze from unsettling content (as they might do when using a phone, for example). Additionally, the anonymity of social VR allows young users to engage in conversations with adults who might otherwise moderate their discussions in the presence of children. Of course, access to mature content is likely part of the allure of social VR for some teenagers.

Impacts of Children on Adults in Social VR

The presence of children in social VR also affects the adult user experience. In a 2020 study by Maloney et al., that involved interviews with 30 social VR users aged 18–65, the behaviour of children was a common concern.[23] The study indicated that young users tend to exhibit immature behaviours in social VR environments, including loud yelling, using slurs and disregarding requests to stop. The prevalence of this type of behaviour in social VR may stem from the content young people consume on platforms like YouTube and Twitch, in which disruptive behaviours are often glorified.[24] As well, research suggests that the social VR platforms popular amongst teenagers, such as *Horizon Worlds*, are failing to provide mechanisms for adequately reporting young users. Online discussions about social VR consistently feature calls from adult users for child-free zones and expressions of concern about the detrimental effect of children's behaviour on adult interactions.

Recently, the VR industry has made moves to abandon the 13 + technology policy, for example, Meta now has preteen accounts for children aged 10–12 and *RecRoom* has 'Junior' accounts for users under 12. Given the potential for psychological, physiological and social harms, as outlined in this chapter, we strongly oppose further expansions of children's use of VR, without more research and better safeguards to protect young users of VR. If the VR industry does not self-correct, policymakers should act quickly to mandate better protections before children's use of VR becomes entrenched, and before the harms are clearly known in hindsight.

Notes

1. We note Meta announced in June 2023 that they are introducing parent-managed accounts for users aged 10–12. See Meta. "Introducing New Parent-Managed Meta accounts for Families." *Meta Quest Blog*, June 17, 2023. https://www.meta.com/en-gb/blog/quest/meta-accounts-parent-managed-families/.
2. Iskander, M., Ogunsola, T., Ramachandran, R., McGowan, R., and Al-Aswad, L. A. "Virtual Reality and Augmented Reality in Ophthalmology: A Contemporary Prospective." *Asia-Pacific Journal of ophthalmology (Philadelphia, PA.)* 10, No. 3 (2021): 244.
3. Rauschenberger, R., and Barakat, B. "Health and Safety of VR Use by Children in an Educational Use Case." In *2020 IEEE Conference on Virtual Reality and 3D User Interfaces (VR)*. IEEE (2020, March): 878–884.
4. Yamada-Rice, D., Mushtaq, F., Woodgate, A., Bosmans, D., Douthwaite, A., Douthwaite, I., ... Whitley, S. "Children and Virtual reality: Emerging possibilities and Challenges" (2017).
5. Since the evolutionary cause for this conflict was typically having eaten some poisonous berries, the drive to vomit makes sense.
6. Stanney, K., Fidopiastis, C., and Foster, L. "Virtual Reality Is Sexist: But It Does Not Have to Be." *Frontiers in Robotics and AI* 7 (2020): 4.

7. Bailey, J. O., and Bailenson, J. N. "Considering Virtual Reality in Children's Lives." *Journal of Children and Media* 11, No. 1 (2017): 107–113.
8. Liao, T., Jennings, N. A., Dell, L., and Collins, C. "Could the Virtual Dinosaur See You? Understanding Children." *Journal for Virtual Worlds Research* 12, No. 2 (2019).
9. Nikken, P., and Peeters, A. L. "Children's Perceptions of Television Reality." *Journal of Broadcasting & Electronic Media* 32, No. 4 (1988): 441–452.
10. Ibid.
11. Maloney, D., Freeman, G., and Robb, A. "Stay Connected in an Immersive World: Why Teenagers Engage in Social Virtual Reality." In *Interaction Design and Children* (2021, June): 69–79.
12. Kaimara, P., Oikonomou, A., and Deliyannis, I. "Could Virtual Reality Applications Pose Real Risks to Children and Adolescents? A Systematic Review of Ethical Issues and Concerns." *Virtual Reality* 26, No. 2 (2022): 697–735.
13. Bean, A. M., Nielsen, R. K., Van Rooij, A. J., and Ferguson, C. J. "Video Game Addiction: The Push to Pathologize Video Games." *Professional Psychology: Research and Practice* 48, No. 5 (2017): 378.
14. Carter, M., Moore, K., Mavoa, J., Gaspard, L., and Horst, H. "Children's Perspectives and Attitudes Towards Fortnite 'Addiction'." *Media International Australia* 176, No. 1 (2020): 138–151.
15. Maloney, D., Freeman, G., and Robb, A. "A Virtual Space for All: Exploring Children's Experience in Social Virtual Reality." In *Proceedings of the Annual Symposium on Computer-Human Interaction in Play* (2020, November): 472–483.
16. Maloney, D., Freeman, G., and Robb, A. "It Is Complicated: Interacting with Children in Social Virtual Reality." In *2020 IEEE Conference on Virtual Reality and 3D User Interfaces Abstracts and Workshops (VRW)*. IEEE (2020, March): 343–347.
17. Fiani, C., Bretin, R., McGill, M., and Khamis, M. "Big Buddy: Exploring Child Reactions and Parental Perceptions Towards a Simulated Embodied Moderating System for Social Virtual Reality." In *Proceedings of the 22nd Annual ACM Interaction Design and Children Conference* (2023, June): 1–13.

18. Jerome, J. "Safe and Secure VR: Policy Issues Impacting Kids' Use of Immersive Tech." *Common Sense Media*, 2021. https://www.commonsensemedia.org/sites/default/files/featured-content/files/safe_and_secure_vr_policy_issues_impacting_kids_final.pdf.
19. Liao, T., Jennings, N. A., Dell, L., and Collins, C. "Could the Virtual Dinosaur See You? Understanding Children." *Journal For Virtual Worlds Research* 12, No. 2 (2019).
20. Druga, S., Williams, R., Breazeal, C., and Resnick, M. "Hey Google Is It OK If I Eat You?: Initial Explorations in Child-Agent Interaction." In *Proceedings of IDC'17*. Stanford, USA (2017): 595–600.
21. For this reason, Meta mentions the ability to 'cast' what a user is seeing in VR to a TV or phone as a safety feature for teens in VR.
22. Centre for Countering Digital Hate. "Horizon Worlds Exposed." *CCDH Report*, March 2023. https://counterhate.com/research/horizon-worlds-exposed/.
23. Maloney, D., Freeman, G., and Robb, A. "It Is Complicated: Interacting with Children in Social Virtual Reality." In *2020 IEEE Conference on Virtual Reality and 3D User Interfaces Abstracts and Workshops (VRW)*. IEEE (2020, March): 343–347.
24. Maloney, D., Freeman, G., and Robb, A. "Stay Connected in an Immersive World: Why Teenagers Engage in Social Virtual Reality." In *Interaction Design and Children* (2021, June): 69–79.

PART II

How Do We Govern?

CHAPTER 5

Designing for Safety, Privacy and Inclusivity in Social VR

Abstract This chapter addresses the imperative of designing social VR environments with safety, privacy and inclusivity at the forefront. It explores principles and best practices proposed by industry stakeholders for creating responsible XR systems. The chapter delves into the privacy concerns posed by biometric and spatial data collection in VR, emphasising the need for continuous consent and informed user choices. It critiques the gendered and ableist biases in current VR design, highlighting the risks of motion sickness and accessibility barriers, and advocates for prioritising accessibility in VR development; the representation of disabilities in avatars; and the importance of including disabled individuals in the design process. Finally, it discusses safety considerations for children, including age-gating and parental controls. The overarching theme is the ethical responsibility of VR developers to create environments that are safe, private and welcoming to all users.

Keywords VR design principles · Privacy and consent · Accessibility and inclusivity · Biometric data · Child safety in VR · Safety by design

J. E. Gray et al., *Governing Social Virtual Reality*,
https://doi.org/10.1007/978-3-031-61831-4_5

Introduction

For social VR, device and system design can provide the foundations for good governance. This chapter explores a range of design principles and practices that social VR companies can adopt to protect users from data harms, improve inclusivity and safeguard children. We review issues relating to data privacy and user consent and argue that the data-intensive nature of VR technologies poses significant privacy risks including the potential for users to be identified through de-identified data. We also examine issues of accessibility in VR, highlighting the current exclusion of diverse bodies in device design and the importance of inclusive development practices to address gender-specific design biases, enable flexibility for users with disabilities and ensure safety features for children.

Data Harms—Designing for Continuous Consent

VR devices are intensive data sensors, presenting new forms of privacy and data risks. Research suggests that extremely granular forms of biometric data can be collected from current VR technologies. As Jeremy Bailenson describes,

> commercial systems typically track body movements 90 times per second...and high-end systems record 18 types of movements across the head and hands. Consequently, spending 20 minutes in a VR simulation leaves just under 2 million unique recordings of body language.[1]

This biometric data, even when anonymised, can be used to identify individual subjects. Miller et al. (2020), for instance, demonstrated that five minutes of VR data collection, with all personally identifiable information removed, could be used to correctly identify an individual using a machine learning algorithm with 95.3% accuracy.[2] This type of biometric VR data has been used to monitor and evaluate workers[3] and considering the growing application of VR and AR technology to workplaces—including factory assembly, logistics and white-collar work—there is a risk that detailed data about an employee's behaviour and bodies could be used to make decisions relating to their employment, raising important questions about user rights to privacy in these contexts.

In addition to biometric data, VR devices also collect and use spatial data. Historically, VR has relied on sensors external to the device to properly calibrate user movement (with sensors tracking the movement of LEDs on the device's controllers and headset, see e.g., the Oculus Rift, HTC Vive). Current XR devices, however, such as the Quest, Vision Pro and Pico, have integrated all sensing componentry into the device itself. These new devices rely on a system of sensors and algorithms (known as Simultaneous Localisation and Mapping, or SLAM) to capture and process data about the built environment to facilitate odometry, that is, changes in the device's position over time. Similar to computer vision in robotics and autonomous vehicles, VR devices make sense of the space around the user by capturing image data from the inbuilt cameras and sensors on the controllers and headset.[4] This type of data collection–what scholar Luke Heemsbergen calls 'biospatial surveillance'–represents a paradigm-changing intensification of how digital devices can track users,[5] and is likely to further intensify with mixed reality devices, such as Meta's Quest and Apple's Vision Pro.

Research shows that there is broad public concern about the privacy implications of VR. For example, a 2022 analysis of 1380 user comments to YouTube videos of Meta's *Connect* conferences held in 2018 and 2019—both of which focused largely on announcing new iterations and design directions of the Oculus VR headset—found that people were highly concerned about data privacy and surveillance implications of Meta's new products.[6] Whilst negative sentiment could be attributed to Meta's history of data-related controversies (for example, the Cambridge Analytica scandal), the study's authors concluded that users were specifically apprehensive about Meta's collection and use of biometric data, some going so far as to express fears of 'mind control'. The study also found that people are anxious about spatial surveillance, for example, in a 2022 study, one participant stated: "And now we have more cameras going into our houses ...like 6 more with this device. What a way to help spy on your families Right Mark [Zuckerberg]?".[7]

Whilst there has been much consternation about VR data harvesting and use by the big tech corporations, third-party app developers also present risks related to user data collection and processing. In an audit of third-party software published on Oculus' app store, Trimananda et al. (2021) found that apps were collecting personally identifiable information that could be used to identify users across different apps and software.[8] By comparing data flows found in network traffic against statements made in the apps' privacy policies, they also concluded that approximately 70% of the data flows had not been properly disclosed to users and 69% were used for purposes unrelated to the core functionality of the apps. As the authors of the study argue, the companies who own and profit from app ecosystems must improve their oversight of and be held accountable for the data collection practices of all parties granted access to VR user data.

For social VR to be deemed trustworthy by users, platforms and developers must obtain their informed consent. Informed consent includes clearly setting out the types of data that will be generated, how it will be used and the justification for each use. Critically, users must also have meaningful opportunities to opt in or out of certain data practices, and their consent must be obtained on an on-going basis as data practices evolve. Research into terms of service agreements suggests that text-based terms of services are not effective at informing users about platform practices and policies,[9] and so VR devices could productively draw from suggestions made by Selinger et al. (2023)[10] for incorporating more active—VR-native—ways of obtaining informed consent, for example, through demonstrations and gestures performed within the immersive environment.

Accessibility by Design—Accounting for Diverse Bodies

In addition to the gendered nature of harassment in social VR as discussed in Chapter 3, VR devices themselves are often sexist. Research has consistently demonstrated that women are at greater risk of motion sickness from VR,[11] primarily due to two design elements—depth cues and interpupillary distance.

To deduce depth, the brain uses motion parallax and shape from shading. Motion parallax is based on the apparent size of the object; if it gets bigger, we deduce that it is getting closer to us. Shape from shading is more complex and is based on how the shading of an object changes very slightly when we move. As social media scholar danah boyd described in her assessment of Meta's Oculus device, "in the real world…both these cues work together to give you a sense of depth. But in virtual reality systems, they're not treated equally".[12] This is because early Oculus devices rely heavily on motion parallax, the proprioceptive technique favoured by men, leading to a much less comfortable experience for women.

The second way that VR hardware discriminates against women is the interpupillary distance (IPD) design. IPD is the distance between the centres of the users' two eyes and is critical in VR because lining up the centre of the eye with the lens within a VR headset is important for comfortable and non-blurry use. Recent research by Kay Stanney and colleagues found that IPD is another driver of gendered differences in motion sickness[13]; the worse the IPD error, the worse the motion sickness.[14] Newer devices permit some adjustments for IPD, however, the range is often not sufficient to address the structural bias towards men. The adjustable IPD range in the Quest 1 is 58–72 mm, and Meta describes 'best' fit as within 2 mm. This means the Quest 1 is 'best' for 98.7% of men but only 94.2% of women.[15] Critically, however, 14.2% of women are more than 4 mm outside the adjustable IPD range versus only 3.3% of men, which leads to more incidents of motion sickness for more women. In other words, the headset is not designed for a diverse range of bodies and many women are being excluded from VR simply because they have not envisioned by designers as user of the system. VR's overwhelmingly male developer (and research[16]) community is designing devices that suit the needs of their bodies.

A bias towards designing for normative male bodies also impacts the use of VR by people with disabilities. Often, VR and virtual worlds are framed as tools for removing barriers for people with disabilities,[17] providing spaces and experiences that are not determined by a person's physical body.[18] But, in practice,VR devices are designed with a body in mind and the kinds of bodies that designers think about are often conceived very narrowly, in patriarchal, able-bodied terms. As summed up by one user who was in a hospital bed and unable to get their VR device to properly calibrate their position— "it [the Quest 2] will not acknowledge me as a person". What 'counts' as a person is circumscribed by the technical limits of the device, underpinned by a wider set of normative attitudes towards the user and the body.

Social theories of disability and VR suggest that rather than thinking about a user's disability as creating a barrier to participating in social VR (as it would be conceived under the now much critiqued 'medical model' of disability), disability should be understood in terms of the *barriers that are created for disabled users by VR technology* (and of the wider sets of social attitudes and biases towards disability that are enfolded into design).[19] This means that when VR devices are designed for able-bodies,[20] VR becomes a 'disabling technology'.[21]

Accessibility, then, should be understood in terms of how the design of digital devices and spaces excludes certain people, as opposed to thinking about how certain people may not 'fit' the technology. If the design focus is on re-creating 'real life' experiences in VR, design choices will often inadvertently recreate accessibility barriers that people with disabilities experience in real life, thus limiting the possibilities for greater accessibility in digital technology. Without careful and sustained consideration of how to include accessibility in design, the benefits of VR for people with disabilities remain hypothetical.

Critically, it is not enough to *imagine* what accessible design choices a person with a disability might need[22]—disabled people should be included in decision-making processes. What a designer might think will benefit a person with a disability may not be helpful[23] and only a narrow range of disabilities might be considered.[24] It is for this reason that disability activists call for the inclusion of people with disabilities in the *design process* rather than just the end product.[25]

Methods such as 'flexible design'[26] and 'multimodal design'[27] are approaches to VR design that allow for adaptable and diverse inputs by a user to ensure that the technology can be adjusted to fit their needs (rather than the user adapting to fit the technology's needs). A flexible system will also allow for greater interoperability with other assistive technologies that people with disabilities rely on.[28] Importantly, flexible design approaches tend to make VR platforms more inclusive overall—if VR technologies are adaptable, more people are likely to enjoy the experience.[29] For instance, someone might prefer to play one-handed because they have a sore arm or they may be more comfortable using subtitles when interacting socially (notably, 80% of people aged 18–24 use TV subtitles, whilst only 10% are deaf or hard of hearing).[30]

Market-leading devices—such as Meta's Quest—include some flexibility features at the device level. However, generally, there has been a failure to properly align these features with the diverse experiences and needs of disabled users. A recent example is the lack of control over avatar height in the Quest platform. The Quest headset uses external facing cameras to scan the environment around the user to situate them as accurately as possible in the virtual environment. This means if you crouch in real life, your avatar crouches in the game. But for wheelchair users and people with limited mobility, this approach makes many Quest games unplayable because the interface is designed to be within reach of a standing user, and a sitting user's view is rendered at crotch-height of the virtual non-player characters. Other issues include seated mode being designed for the comfort of the normative body type rather than for the inclusion of those for whom sitting is a necessity and colour correction options useful to only one type of colour-blindness (monochromacy). Overall, current approaches to design flexibility do not attend to the diversity of lived experiences.

As the ecosystem for VR experiences grows, third-party accessibility design practices will increasingly determine the user experience across VR platforms. The market leader in VR, Meta, provides third-party software developers *optional* 'best practices' for designing for accessibility. Meta does not provide solutions that are baked into the hardware or tools for developers. This approach pushes accessibility choices onto app developers, requiring each development team to 'reinvent the wheel' when it comes to accessibility. This can see accessibility considerations falling victim to the resource constraints (and often precarious economic realities) of the software development industry. Apple's Vision Pro promises a more productive solution—providing the software development tools that allow developers to design *for* disability (for instance, development tools that allow third-party developers to easily change text-based prompts to audio).[31]

Although accessibility requires more than just the inclusion of diverse avatars—because a person with a disability will never see themselves meaningfully represented in VR if they are unable to use the technology in the first place—*representation* of people with disabilities in VR avatars is also important for inclusive social VR. Certainly, some people with disabilities will not want to have their disabilities reflected in their avatars. However, a study by Zhang et al. (2022) found that many disabled users see avatar creation as a means of authentic identity expression and community-building with other disabled users.[32] Beyond work on social VR, a wider body of research on social media—such as on emojis—suggests that visual/image-based forms of communication fulfil an important social function when they act as signifiers of affect, identity, emotion and sociality[33] (and indeed, there are emojis that represent a range of disabilities available on iOS and Android devices).[34]

To date, there is limited avatar diversity for people with disabilities in social VR—most platforms do not offer any disability-related avatar features. Meta's avatar system is the only exception with the option for including a limited range of assistive devices in avatar customisation (outside of other objects that may fall under the umbrella of disability, such as glasses).[35] Adding a bigger range of avatar customisation features—including assistive devices and the option for representing non-visible disabilities such as autism—would be a welcome industry change.[36] Representation in social VR also intersects with issues of gender. For instance, research by ILMxLabs[37] (the immersive entertainment arm of the LucasFilm production company) reported that limits on the ability to customise avatars beyond the male–female binary triggered a trans user's anxiety and physical nausea.

Beyond the symbolic benefits, representation options in social VR can also play a functional role. Avatar customisation might allow for users to create multiple avatar 'loadouts', which could be used in specific social contexts. For example, in *VRChat*, the ability to customise aspects like avatar hands has been a central way in which the Deaf community has learnt, taught and performed VR ASL (a simplified version of American Sign Language).[38]

Safety by Design–Considerations for Children

As children are highly vulnerable users in VR, platforms have a greater responsibility to implement safety by design features for their protection. Currently, many platforms age-gate content and apply additional restrictions on child/teen accounts. For example, *Horizon Worlds* includes accounts for teens aged 13 to 17, which come with additional safety features such as making accounts private by default, prohibiting teens from entering worlds with mature content, enabling voice mode by default and limiting interactions between teens and unknown adults.[39] Meta also has some VR parental supervision tools that let parents/guardians lock these safety features, monitor the time spent playing and block access to specific apps.[40] As discussed in Chapter 4, providing parents with more capacity to oversee and participate in children's VR use is needed if we are to protect young users who are still developing important cognitive and impulse control skills.

In June 2023, Meta announced the addition of preteen accounts for children aged 10 to 12, with parental controls over VR content, including the ability to "manage how long their preteen can use the headset each day and schedule breaks from their device".[41] Currently, Meta's preteen accounts do not have access to social VR. *RecRoom*, however, has 'junior' accounts for users under 12. Users with these accounts cannot use voice or text chat, they are provided unique random usernames and they cannot access user-generated content with frightening or mature themes.[42] For *RecRoom,* age verification involves a $1 payment,[43] which creates a moment of friction for children seeking to surreptitiously access the platform—they must first get access to a credit card. If VR platforms continue to pursue younger users, more of these types of design interventions will be needed to enable parental oversight.

Notes

1. Bailenson, J. "Protecting Nonverbal Data Tracked in Virtual Reality." *JAMA Pediatrics* 172, No. 10 (2018): 905–906.
2. Miller, M. R., Herrera, F., Jun, H., Landay, J. A., and Bailenson, J. N. "Personal Identifiability of User Tracking Data During Observation of 360-Degree VR Video." *Scientific Reports* 10, No. 1 (2020): 17404.
3. Carter, M., and Egliston, B. "What Are the Risks of Virtual Reality Data? Learning Analytics, Algorithmic Bias and a Fantasy of Perfect Data." *New Media & Society* 25, No. 3 (2023): 485–504.
4. Egliston, B., and Carter, M. "Critical Questions for Facebook's Virtual Reality: Data, Power and the Metaverse." *Internet Policy Review* 10, No. 4 (2021).
5. Heesmbergen, L. "Apple's Vision of Ourselves." *Critical Augmented and Virtual Reality Research Network (CAVRN)* (2024). https://cavrn.org/apples-vision-of-ourselves/
6. Egliston, B., and Carter, M. "Oculus Imaginaries: The Promises and Perils of Facebook's Virtual Reality." *New Media & Society* 24, No. 1 (2022): 70–89.
7. Ibid.
8. Trimananda, R., Le, H., Cui, H., Ho, J. T., Shuba, A., and Markopoulou, A. "{OVRseen}: Auditing Network Traffic and Privacy Policies in Oculus {VR}." In *31st USENIX Security Symposium (USENIX Security 22)* (2022): 3789–3806.
9. Waldman, A. E. "Privacy, Notice, and Design." *Stanford Technology Law Review* 21 (2018): 129.
10. Selinger, E., Altman, E., and Foster, S. "Eye-Tracking in Virtual Reality: A Visceral Notice Approach for Protecting Privacy." *Privacy Studies Journal* 2 (2023): 1–34.

11. Munafo, J., et al. "The Virtual Reality Head-Mounted Display Oculus Rift Induces Motion Sickness and Is Sexist in Its Effects." *Experimental Brain Research* 235 (2017): 889–901.
12. See boyd, d. "Is the Oculus Rift Sexist." *Quartz*, March 28, 2014. https://qz.com/192874/is-the-oculus-rift-designed-to-be-sexist.
13. Stanney, K., Fidopiastis, C., and Foster, L. "Virtual Reality Is Sexist: But It Does Not Have to Be." *Frontiers in Robotics and AI* 7 (2020): 4.
14. Stanney et al.'s study included measurements one hour post exposure, so this was not trivial motion sickness but motion sickness with a lasting effect upon the user.
15. The ANSUR II (Anthropometric Survey) is a public data set created by the US Army in 2012, based on measurements of US army soldiers and reservists. See Heaney, D. "Data Suggests Oculus Rift S IPD Range 'Best' for Just Half of Adults." *UploadVR*, April 5, 2019. https://www.uploadvr.com/data-suggests-oculus-rift-s-ipd-range-best-for-around-half-ofadults/#:~:text=One%20of%20those%20measures%20is%20interpupillary%20distance.&text=The%20data%20shows%20Quest's%20mechanical,men%20and%2043%25%20of%20women.
16. Peck, T. C., Sockol, L. E., and Hancock, S. M. "Mind the Gap: The Underrepresentation of Female Participants and Authors in Virtual Reality Research." *IEEE Transactions on Visualization and Computer Graphics* 26, No. 5 (2020): 1945–1954.
17. Hoshaw, L. "Affordable Virtual Reality Opens New Worlds For People With Disabilities." *NPR*, October 22, 2015. https://www.npr.org/sections/health-shots/2015/10/22/450573400/affordable-virtual-reality-opens-new-worlds-for-people-with-disabilities.
18. Fox, D., and Thornton, I. G. "White Paper: The IEEE Global Initiative on Ethics of Extended Reality (XR) Report—Extended Reality (XR) Ethics and Diversity, Inclusion, and Accessibility." *The IEEE Global Initiative on Ethics of Extended Reality (XR) Report—Extended Reality (XR) Ethics and Diversity, Inclusion, and Accessibility* (2022): 1–25.
19. Knight, J. "Cognitive Barries in VR and Beyond—Axe-con 2021." Recorded talk uploaded to YouTube from AxeCon 2021, *YouTube*, November 5, 2022. https://www.youtube.com/watch?v=BRD6mBLDR3w.

20. Egliston, B., and Carter, M. "Critical Questions for Facebook's Virtual Reality: Data, Power and the Metaverse." *Internet Policy Review* 10, No. 4 (2021).
21. Gerling, K., and Spiel, K. "A Critical Examination of Virtual Reality Technology in the Context of the Minority Body." In *Proceedings of the 2021 CHI Conference on Human Factors in Computing Systems* (2021, May): 1–14.
22. Bennett, C. L., and Rosner, D. K. "The Promise of Empathy: Design, Disability, and Knowing the Other." In *Proceedings of the 2019 CHI Conference on Human Factors in Computing Systems* (2019, May): 1–13.
23. Felix, A. "An Accessible, Disability-Inclusive Metaverse." *Accessibility, Information and Communication Technologies* (2022). https://www.edf-feph.org/anaccessible-disability-inclusive-metaverse/.
24. Hughes, L. "The Metaverse at Work Is Going to Alienate Your Disabled Employees, Here's Why." *TechRadar*, October 29, 2022. https://www.techradar.com/news/the-metaverse-at-work-is-going-to-alienate-your-disabled-employees-heres-why.
25. Costanza-Chock, S. *Design Justice: Community-Led Practices to Build the Worlds We Need.* The MIT Press, 2020. See also Knight, J. "Cognitive Barriers in VR and Beyond." Recorded talk uploaded to YouTube from AxeCon 2021. *YouTube*, November 5, 2021. https://www.youtube.com/watch?v=BRD6mBLDR3w.
26. Meta Quest. "Oculus Connect 5, Accessibility: Build, Influence and Grow Adoption over the Next 5 Years in VR." *YouTube*, September 28, 2018. https://www.youtube.com/watch?v=JzCFhCzvL7U.
27. W3C Working Group. "XR Accessibility User Requirements". *W3C*, August 25, 2021. https://www.w3.org/TR/xaur/.
28. Carine, M., Moledo, A., and Naughton, C. "Plug and Pray? A Disability Perspective on Artificial Intelligence, Automated Decision Making and Immersive Technologies." *European Disability Forum*, 2018. https://www.edf-feph.org/content/uploads/2020/12/edf-emerging-tech-report-accessible.pdf.
29. Dick, E. "Public Policy for the Metaverse: Key Takeaways from the 2021 AR/VR Policy Conference." *ITIF*, November 15, 2021. https://itif.org/publications/2021/11/15/public-policy-metaverse-key-takeaways-2021-arvr-policy-conference/.

30. Youngs, I. "Young Viewers Prefer TV Subtitles, Research Suggests." *BBC News*, November 15, 2021. https://www.bbc.com/news/entertainment-arts-59259964.
31. Apple Developer, "Create Accessible Spatial Experiences." *WWDC2023.* Accessed July 15, 2023. https://developer.apple.com/videos/play/wwdc2023/10034.
32. Zhang, K., Deldari, E., Lu, Z., Yao, Y., and Zhao, Y. ""It's Just Part of Me:" Understanding Avatar Diversity and Self-Presentation of People with Disabilities in Social Virtual Reality." In *Proceedings of the 24th International ACM SIGACCESS Conference on Computers and Accessibility* (2022, October): 1–16.
33. Stark, L., and Crawford, K. "The Conservatism of Emoji: Work, Affect, and Communication." *Social Media + Society* 1, No. 2 (2015): 2056305115604853.
34. Pope, N., "Inclusive Emoji Update Sees Better Representation of Disability." *Disability Support Guide.* Accessed August 1, 2023. https://www.disabilitysupportguide.com.au/talking-disability/inclusive-emoji-update-sees-better-representation-of-disability.
35. Ibid.
36. Ibid.
37. Wong, A., Gillis, H., and Peck, B. "VR Accessibility: Survey for People with Disabilities" (2017).
38. Zhang, K., Deldari, E., Lu, Z., Yao, Y., and Zhao, Y. "It's Just Part of Me:" Understanding Avatar Diversity and Self-Presentation of People with Disabilities in Social Virtual Reality." In *Proceedings of the 24th International ACM SIGACCESS Conference on Computers and Accessibility* (2022, October): 1–16.
39. Meta. "Welcoming Teens to Meta Horizon Worlds in the US and Canada." *Meta Newsroom*, April 18, 2023. https://about.fb.com/news/2023/04/horizon-worlds-teen-expansion-us-canada/.
40. Meta. "Introducing Future VR Parental Supervision Tools to Help Support Families." *Meta Quest Blog*, March 17, 2022. https://www.meta.com/en-gb/blog/quest/introducing-future-vr-parental-supervision-tools-to-help-support-families/.
41. Meta. "Introducing New Parent-Managed Meta Accounts for Families." *Meta Quest Blog*, June 17, 2023. https://www.meta.com/en-gb/blog/quest/meta-accounts-parent-managed-families/.

42. RecRoom. "A Parent's Guide to Rec Room." *RecRoom*. https://recroom.com/parents-guide.
43. RecRoom. "Junior Accounts." *RecRoom*. https://recroom.zendesk.com/hc/en-us/articles/4426900227735-Junior-Accounts.

CHAPTER 6

Trust and Safety in Social VR: Current Industry Practices

Abstract This chapter reviews the spectrum of moderation techniques currently deployed across social VR platforms to tackle user conduct and content issues, distinguishing between reactive and proactive strategies. It evaluates common reactive safety features like in-app reporting, vote kicking, blocking and user monitoring, noting their limitations and the burden they place on victims. The chapter also explores proactive measures, including personal boundaries, voice controls and community norms, aimed at preventing harassment and abuse. It underscores the challenges of balancing user safety with engagement and the necessity for a multifaceted approach that combines both reactive and proactive elements to foster pro-social behaviour and ensure a safe VR environment.

Keywords Social VR moderation · Reactive safety measures · Proactive safety features · User safety and engagement · Community norms and behaviour · Trust and safety · Safety by design

J. E. Gray et al., *Governing Social Virtual Reality*,
https://doi.org/10.1007/978-3-031-61831-4_6

Introduction

There are a range of tools and features that current social VR platforms provide to moderate user conduct and content. These measures operate as a form of self-governance by the VR industry, with each platform aiming to enforce a specific set of rules and principles outlined in their Terms of Service and Community Guidelines, which can vary across services and jurisdictions in the context of specific legal, social and economic conditions. Under the umbrella of 'Trust and Safety', current industry practices tend to fit within one of two overarching modes—*reactive* mechanisms that can be used in response to platform rule-breaking and *proactive* mechanisms that seek to prevent rule-breaking. In this chapter, we provide an overview of the most common of these—drawing from social VR platforms (*Horizon Worlds, RecRoom, VR Chat, AltspaceVR*) and popular multiplayer VR games (*EchoVR*, *Demeo*, *PopulationOne*)—assessing their strengths and weaknesses as measures for effectively protecting VR users from harm. We evaluate the reactive safety measures of in-app reporting, vote kicking, blocking and monitoring, and the proactive mechanisms of player boundaries, voice modulation and tools for establishing community norms. As our analysis shows, there is no single feature that acts as a silver bullet for mitigating harm in social VR. Indeed, we argue that effective content and conduct moderation must include a combination of reactive and proactive safety features.

Reactive Safety—Reporting, Voting, Blocking and Monitoring

Reactive safety features give users the ability to respond *after* an instance of harassment, abuse or other content or conduct harm has occurred. Reactive measures do not prevent harm and they tend to place the burden of managing safety on victims, who are most commonly women and other marginalised users. As well, across platforms, these features are often not sufficiently easy to access, particularly during an embodied and transient interaction in social VR.

In-App Reporting

One of the most common moderation strategies used by most, if not all, social VR platforms is the in-app report, which allows a user to select another user in VR and report them for violating codes of conduct, community guidelines or terms of service. How in-app reporting is implemented varies across platforms. *Horizon Worlds* has the strongest in-app reporting system as the device continually records two minutes of content. When a report is initiated, the previous two minutes are saved and uploaded with the report. In contrast, *VRChat*, *RecRoom* and *EchoVR* do not have any built-in recording tools. To make a recording on those platforms, users need to have installed third-party tools[1] or device-recording features and have them activated prior to the incident. For instance, PCVR users can install software such as NVIDIA Shadowplay, which continually records the last 10 minutes of gameplay. Notably, *VRChat* requires that the reports include a video that is at least 2 minutes in length to "show context for the situation described" despite not providing a recording function.

Due to the ephemeral nature of social interactions in VR, in-app recording is the gold standard for effective reporting systems. Determining the optimal length for automated recording is not straightforward, however. *Horizon Worlds*' two-minute recording window may not adequately capture prolonged harassment episodes. Extended recording is also necessary for accurate human-review of reports, because otherwise bad actors might mass report marginalised users as a form of harassment, despite those users not having done anything wrong when viewed in the context of a larger dispute.[2]

To be effective, in-app reporting must also be sufficiently easy to use. *RecRoom*, for example, includes a 'pointing gesture' that allows users to easily select another user in order to mute, block or report them.[3] They also have a 'Recent Players' list, which provides a list of players that users have encountered during their current session. This means that users can report someone even if that person has already left the room. *RecRoom* provides a similarly intuitive and easy to use reporting function through a 'Talk to the Hand' mute gesture. If a user holds their hand out with palm facing another user for approximately one second, that user is muted and removed from their view, with further options available through the wrist menu (such as muting or reporting the user). This mimics a real-life gesture and is therefore easy to use, easy to recall in the moment and quickly effective, helping better protect users generally and supporting marginalised users to feel more confident in social VR despite a higher risk of harassment. In their review of safety design in social VR, Zheng et al. (2023) emphasised the need for more natural reactive safety measures with easy triggers, suggesting, for instance, a 'covering ears' gesture to temporarily mute all audio.[4]

Another critical element of effective in-app reporting is transparency regarding outcomes. The Santa Clara Principles on Transparency and Accountability in Content Moderation set out "minimum standards that tech platforms must meet in order to provide adequate transparency and accountability around their efforts to take down user-generated content or suspend accounts that violate their rules".[5] Included in these standards is the requirement that "users who flag content should be presented with a log of content they have reported and the outcomes of moderation processes". Current approaches to feedback on reporting vary across platforms. *RecRoom* provides feedback to some users, but on an ad hoc basis; *Horizon Worlds* provides updates on the process but not outcome, whilst *VRChat* and *Altspace* VR do not provide information about the outcome of a report as a policy. As discussed in Chapter 2, advising users—particularly those who are the victims of harassment—about the outcome of their complaints is critical for creating community norms against harassing and hateful conduct. By not doing so, platforms are at risk of implicitly encouraging antisocial behaviours.[6] As one frustrated *VRChat* user commented online, "I stopped filing moderation tickets when I realised nothing was happening". Failure to properly inform users about the outcome of their complaint can create a perception that reports are not actioned, and the platform does not prioritise user safety.[7]

A common limitation of in-app reporting within social VR platforms is that, whilst it typically works well for behaviours that explicitly violate platform rules such as pornographic or racist acts, it does not work as well for 'borderline' incidents, such as continually redirecting conversations towards sexual or racial themes. This can create a reductive binary classification of behaviour in social VR, leaving users without recourse for addressing behaviours that are merely bothersome or toxic. Peer-review rating systems (a proactive mode of moderation), common in online gaming, can go some way to addressing this limitation. *VRChat's* 'Trust System', for instance, assigns trust ranks to users, ranging from 'Visitor' to 'Trusted User', based on numerous factors, including time spent in the app without reports of misconduct (more detailed specifics are undisclosed to prevent malicious gaming of the system). Other VR users are then able to set their proactive safety settings to, for example, mute users with a low trust rank.[8] For *VRChat*, the trust system also provides the platform a way to evaluate user reports: reports from known, trusted users can be automatically enforced, as though they were administered by a *VRChat* employee.[9]

Vote Kick

Horizon Worlds, *RecRoom* and *VRChat* offer 'vote kick' features, such as the 'Poll to Remove' in *Horizon Worlds* described in Chapter 2. This community-based moderation tool allows a user to suggest the removal of another user from the space, with the rest of the users in the space voting to agree or disagree. Compared to reporting, the advantage of this feature is that it leads to immediate action against bad behaviour and can address annoying or antisocial behaviour that may not violate a specific community guideline. As a community-based intervention, it can also influence the development of pro-social norms. However, as with the Soapstone Comedy Club incident described in Chapter 3, vote kick features are open to misuse. In that case, a group of users exhibiting racist behaviour voted out a Latino man and a journalist who commented on the incident. Similar complaints about the abuse of the vote kick systems are widespread in online discussions. For instance, a *RecRoom* user stated, "recently a group of players engaged in sexually explicit actions and vote-kicked me before I could report them". Such misuse of tools by certain players is an established pattern of griefing and online harassment, particularly in gaming cultures in which vote kick features are common.[10] Vote kick can also turn into spam during large events, with players reporting others without valid reasons. To combat this, *Horizon Worlds* now grants event creators the option to disable the vote kick feature during specific events.[11]

Blocking

Most online social spaces—including social media, messaging, gaming and VR—provide users the ability to block other users. In VR, however, the implementation and effectiveness of blocking are very different than for 2D media. In social media, for example, it is possible to entirely remove another user from one's online experience. Once blocked, the user's profile and content will no longer appear in the social media feed of the user who blocked them. In VR, on the other hand, if a user blocks another user, both users will often still be present in the virtual space but with reduced avatar visibility and limitations on direct communication. In

RecRoom, for instance, if a user blocks another user, they can no longer hear them and their avatar becomes translucent from the perspective of the user who blocked them. For other users in the environment, the appearance of the blocker and blocked user does not change, and they can both still be heard. The blocking player also becomes muted and transparent from the perspective of the blocked user, but both know that they are still present in the space. Because blocked players retain a social presence, this creates opportunities for continued harassment: a harasser can still impose an unwanted virtual presence as a means of exerting control or influence over another user, such as by continuing to follow them around. Users variously described this as 'eerie', 'annoying' and 'defeating', even when the harasser's avatar was completely invisible (such as in *VRChat*).

Horizon Worlds initially prevented blocked players from being in the same private world, but this meant that victims of harassment were often forced to choose between blocking a harassing user and remaining in a space.[12] Generally, the most effective approach to blocking in VR involves providing users with control and choice over the way in which blocking is implemented across different social situations. We identify four basic degrees of blocking for social VR: blocking audio (muting), blocking avatars (making another users' avatar invisible, but still staying in the same environment), hiding avatars (make your own avatar invisible to another user) and blocking user (mute and block, stopping them from being able to be in the same private world).

As examined in part one of this book, harassment in VR can be highly distressing, and requiring users to navigate complex menus or system settings to protect themselves *whilst being harassed* places an unfair burden on the victims of harassment. This is particularly difficult when there are multiple people harassing someone, as each user needs to be blocked individually, leaving a user open to harassment whilst they take steps to block people one by one. The safest option for most users then becomes to log out, which can then prevent them from blocking, reporting or taking other remediating actions. To address this common limitation of blocking mechanisms, *VRChat* has 'Safe Mode', which provides "a shortcut to immediately disable all features on all users around you". If a user pulls the trigger and presses the menu button on both controllers at the same time, all safety features are enabled at once: all other users in the space will be hidden and muted. This gives a user time to individually block or report, mute, change their safety settings or move to another area in the space. *Horizon Worlds* has a similar feature called ‘Safe Zone’ which can be accessed from the wrist menu. As with reporting, to be effective, blocking features must be highly intuitive and easy to use, so that a user can act quickly to protect themselves from harassment. *RecRoom’s* talk to the hand gesture is an exemplary model of this type of intuitive design that helps to keep users safe in social VR.

Live Monitoring

Due to the ephemeral and synchronous nature of VR conduct, social VR platforms often utilise human and AI moderators who are present in the environment. In *Horizon Worlds*, there are visible community guides (who are a mix of volunteers and employees) in public spaces, as well as paid undercover moderators who are either visible but not identified as moderators or completely invisible to other users. In *VRChat*, moderators do not interact with users but do monitor conduct in public spaces. *RecRoom* utilises volunteer moderators in public rooms, who are players with access to additional tools (such as being able to remove players) and requires content creators to moderate the spaces they create. Their code of conduct specifically states: “If you create a room, you are responsible for making sure it doesn’t devolve into a toxic mess”. *Horizon Worlds* also has a ‘governance best practices’ guide for creators.[13]

There are trade-offs between opting for either visible or hidden human moderators. Visible moderators can help establish norms for appropriate behaviours by cautioning players who are on the verge of violating conduct rules and shaping pro-social behaviours.[14] Their presence can serve as a deterrent and allow for immediate intervention during an incident. However, moderators need to be well trained and willing to take action to protect other users. In a widely reported 2021 incident where a *Horizon Worlds* beta tester was subjected to sexual harassment, one of the key issues was that the visible moderator failed to act. The user explained, “even after I reported, and eventually blocked the assaulter, the guide in the plaza did and said nothing. He moved himself far across the map as if to say, you’re on your now”.[15] Since then, there have been calls for better training for live moderators, as well as clearer rules for when and in what situations human moderators will intervene.[16]

It can be hard for even well-trained moderators to effectively address all types of harassment, particularly if it comes from individuals who have learned to refrain from engaging in misconduct when a moderator is present. Hidden moderators can address this problem, but they also present an issue for user privacy. In scenarios where two friends are conversing alone in a public space, arguably, there is a reasonable expectation of privacy and an assumption that their conversation should not be subjected to surveillance. The use of hidden moderators in private spaces is highly likely to conflict with social VR user expectations of privacy.

As discussed in Chapter 2, in social VR, automated, or AI, moderation can also be used to filter certain keywords and block content, such as via the software *ToxMod* used by *RecRoom*.[17] Whilst AI is fast and well developed for asynchronous social media, it is limited in its capacity to deal with context, conduct and evolving community norms in social VR. Research has demonstrated that AI-based moderation can sometimes detect toxic behaviour in real time and, as it improves, there is potential for it to be applied to complement other social VR safety features, such as reporting and live moderation.[18] There are growing calls in research regarding social VR safety for non-playable character (NPC)-based AI moderators who intervene when users are acting inappropriately, providing visible conduct moderation in a way that is theorised to help shape pro-social behaviour.[19]

Proactive Safety—Boundaries, Voice Controls and Community Norms

Proactive trust and safety features seek to prevent the occurrence of harassment, abuse and other content and conduct harms in social VR. In addition to being preventive, in contrast to reactive features, proactive features typically also have the advantage of affording users the ability to determine their own approach to, and level of, personal safety in immersive spaces.

Personal Boundary

After Jordan Belamire recounted her experience of sexual assault in *QuiVr*, as described in Chapter 3, *QuiVr* developers introduced an enhanced 'personal bubble' feature, which causes other users' virtual hands and avatars to automatically vanish when they invade a user's personal space. This feature has since been adopted as a standard across most social VR platforms, although approaches to implementation vary. *VRChat*, for example, has a non-adjustable 'personal space' feature set by default. In contrast, *RecRoom* allows users to modify their 'ignore bubble', which defaults to roughly two virtual feet. In *Horizon Worlds*, avatars come with a two-foot personal boundary, offering three settings: 'on for non-friends' (default), 'on for everyone' or 'off'.

Comfortable interpersonal distance is not uniform; it fluctuates based on variables such as avatar size, movement, the user's sense of embodiment and demographic factors like age and gender.[20] It also shifts with personal preferences for social intimacy. Whilst research suggests that a four-foot default may be broadly appropriate, findings also indicate that neurodivergent individuals may prefer more space,[21] and that cultural differences play a role in space intimacy preferences.[22] Thus, the most effective boundaries in social VR are those that users can tailor to their own needs, including allowing different settings for friends versus strangers.

A limitation of personal boundaries is that they can hinder collaboration in virtual spaces by preventing close interaction, such as sharing objects or gestures like high-fives or handshakes. To reconcile safety and functionality, a temporary deactivation of personal boundaries—such as for five minutes or a single session—could be an effective solution to this issue, one that recognises that user safety, and need for safety features, is something that changes over time. However, in all cases, reactivation should be easy and intuitive. *QuiVR's* developers have implemented a 'power gesture' to activate the personal boundary, a symbolic and empowering action enabling instant reclamation of personal space.[23] As media discussions around safety in social VR increase, there is a push to standardise such empowering gestures across platforms.[24]

Voice Controls

All social VR platforms facilitate communication by voice, but one of the limitations of voice (versus text) is that it can convey information about a speaker's identity. For marginalised users, particularly women, this makes interacting with other users through voice chat risky.[25] Research has consistently found that women overwhelmingly do not use voice chat in online games and avoid games that require it.[26] One inadvertent consequence of this is the reinforced false perception that games are a male-only space, and that competitive games that require voice chat for competition are only appealing to men. This is not the case; these games are simply only safe for men. To limit gender-based exclusion on its platform, *RecRoom* offers microphone settings that enable users to change the pitch of their voice, which can help women 'gender mask'. *EchoVR* also has a similar 'voice modulation' setting so users can lower their voice pitch. There are also numerous third-party voice changer applications which are popular within the *VRChat* community with additional uses such as in role-play.

Whilst *Horizon Worlds* does not provide a voice manipulation that can gender mask, it does have voice safety features that proactively mute or garble the voices of all people who you are not following. Meta explains, "with voice mode turned to garble voices, the voices of people you aren't following will become unintelligible, pleasant sounds".[27] What is particularly innovative about this feature is that "if you want to hear what people are saying with voice mode to set garble, you can hold either controller near your ear to temporarily hear them" or use a 'cupped ear' gesture. Like *RecRoom's* reporting gestures, this intuitive and easily accessible feature empowers users with flexibility in how they protect themselves from potentially unsafe speech and embodies the principle of providing users more control and choice over their safety levels in social VR.

Community Norms

As discussed in Chapter 2, distinguishing between private, semi-public and public spaces is a form of safety by design because the distinction allows for different moderation practices and community norms to be applied and developed across different types of spaces.[28] Private spaces are virtual worlds that can only be joined by people already connected as friends (such as on *VRChat*), or only if they are given explicit invites (such as *RecRoom's* 'Dorm', *Horizon World's* 'Personal Space'). Typically, the owner of a private space has increased power to moderate the space, such as being able to mute a user (for everyone) and remove a user from the space entirely. In *Horizon Worlds*, users can set rules that are in addition to the *Code of Conduct for Virtual Experiences*, such as 'no profanity or swearing', 'don't criticise' and 'be kind and courteous'.[29] These kinds of private spaces can be much safer for users, because they do not enable social experiences with strangers.

Semi-public spaces, such as 'members-only worlds' in *Horizon Worlds*, are similar to private spaces but rather than needing to be invited to the space, you can join if you are already a member of the community. As of July 2023, on *Horizon Worlds*, this feature is currently only in testing and is restricted to community sizes of 150. Just as in real life, these semi-private spaces offer greater protection for users in comparison to public spaces. Creators can set additional rules, have governance responsibilities over the space and access to a moderation dashboard to set and enforce the spaces' rules. *RecRoom* has a similar 'Clubs' feature, with creators responsible for the moderation of their clubs.

Public spaces are those that are available to all users on a platform. Some public, user-created spaces in *Horizon Worlds* have 'house rules', for example, the Soapstone Comedy Club a VR comedy club has its house rules (which include, for example, no sexually graphic topics) projected on the wall next to the comedy stage. However, as discussed in Chapter 2, in a public space, users will encounter people they do not know, making these spaces less safe generally and in need of the most comprehensive and multidimensional moderation modalities. What is also critical for public and semi-public space is that the governance of the space is explicitly clear to users. It should be clear who is responsible for moderating that space. The *RecRoom* code of conduct explicitly states that "rooms are behaviour", that is, a room is an extension of the player who created them, and that "room ownership is an active responsibility...If you can't devote some energy into proactively checking on your room (e.g., maybe you're going on vacation) consider making it private for the duration, or finding a trusted co-owner".

The landscape of safety features and moderation modalities in social VR platforms is diverse, reflecting the evolving nature of VR technology and its intersection with ethical considerations and legal standards. This chapter has delved into existing reactive and proactive safety measures across various social VR platforms, shedding light on their strengths and weaknesses as tools for preventing harm. Reactive safety measures, such as in-app reporting, vote kicking, blocking and monitoring, provide users with tools to respond after instances of harassment or misconduct. However, these measures often place the burden of managing safety on victims and may not be easily accessible during transient interactions in social VR. This is why a comprehensive safety net for users of social VR requires a combination of both proactive and reactive mechanism, designed and implemented to support pro-social platform cultures.

Notes

1. Use of this software is not possible on enclosed systems such as Meta's *Quest*.
2. Maloney, D., Freeman, G., and Robb, A. "Stay Connected in an Immersive World: Why Teenagers Engage in Social Virtual Reality." In *Interaction Design and Children* (2021, June): 69–79. Maloney and colleagues report a player being subjected to homophobic slurs and reported by the harasser, despite having not done anything wrong.
3. Rec Room. "How to Rec Room—Comfort and Moderation—VR Players." YouTube, August 24, 2018. https://www.youtube.com/watch?v=T5lw58uruCw.
4. Zheng, Q., Xu, S., Wang, L., Tang, Y., Salvi, R. C., Freeman, G., and Huang, Y. "Understanding Safety Risks and Safety Design in Social VR Environments." *Proceedings of the ACM on Human-Computer Interaction* 7(CSCW1) (2023): 1–37.
5. See Santa Clara Principles Coalition. "The Santa Clara Principles on Transparency and Accountability in Content Moderation". https://santaclaraprinciples.org/history/.
6. Fiani, C., Bretin, R., McGill, M., and Khamis, M. "Big Buddy: Exploring Child Reactions and Parental Perceptions Towards a Simulated Embodied Moderating System for Social Virtual Reality." In *Proceedings of the 22nd Annual ACM Interaction Design and Children Conference* (2023 June): 1–13.
7. Schulenberg, K., Li, L., Freeman, G., Zamanifard, S., and McNeese, N. J. "Towards Leveraging AI-Based Moderation to Address Emergent Harassment in Social Virtual Reality." In *Proceedings of the 2023 CHI Conference on Human Factors in Computing Systems* (2023, April): 1–17.
8. Kou, Y., and Gui, X. "Flag and Flaggability in Automated Moderation: The Case of Reporting Toxic Behavior in an Online Game Community." In *Proceedings of the 2021 CHI Conference on Human Factors in Computing Systems* (2021, May): 1–12.
9. This is similar to YouTube's 'trusted flagger' program implemented from 2012–2022, which weighted some users' reports higher than others. This program has been replaced with AI-based moderation, although they retain a priority flagger program for certain government agencies, industry partners and NGOs.

10. Dibbell, J. "A Rape in Cyberspace: How an Evil Clown, a Haitian Trickster Spirit, Two Wizards, and a Cast of Dozens Turned a Database into a Society." *JulianDibbell.com*, December 23, 1993 (May 2021). http://www.juliandibbell.com/texts/bungle_vv.html.
11. Meta. "Meta Horizon Worlds v91 Release Notes." *Meta Quest Blog*, January 7, 2023. https://www.meta.com/en-gb/blog/quest/meta-horizon-worlds-v91-release-notes/.
12. More granular controls were added to the platform in a July 2023 update. Meta. "Meta Horizon Worlds v119 Release Notes." *Meta Quest Blog*, July 18, 2023. https://www.meta.com/en-gb/blog/quest/meta-horizon-worlds-v119-release-notes/.
13. Meta. "Members-Only Worlds Governance Best Practices in Meta Horizon Worlds." *Meta Quest Help*, December 2022. https://www.meta.com/en-gb/help/quest/articles/horizon/safety-and-privacy-in-horizon-worlds/governance-members-only-worlds/.
14. Blackwell, L., Ellison, N., Elliott-Deflo, N., and Schwartz, R. "Harassment in Social Virtual Reality: Challenges for Platform Governance." *Proceedings of the ACM on Human-Computer Interaction* 3(CSCW) (2019): 1–25.
15. Duffield, W. "A Grope in Meta's Space." *CATO Institute*, December 28, 2021. https://www.cato.org/commentary/grope-metas-space.
16. Schulenberg, K., Li, L., Freeman, G., Zamanifard, S., and McNeese, N. J. "Towards Leveraging AI-Based Moderation to Address Emergent Harassment in Social Virtual Reality." In *Proceedings of the 2023 CHI Conference on Human Factors in Computing Systems* (2023, April): 1–17.
17. Kou, Y., and Gui, X. "Flag and Flaggability in Automated Moderation: The Case of Reporting Toxic Behavior in an Online Game Community." In *Proceedings of the 2021 CHI Conference on Human Factors in Computing Systems* (2021, May): 1–12; Stoop, W., Kunneman, F., van den Bosch, A., and Miller, B. "Detecting Harassment in Real-Time as Conversations Develop." In *Proceedings of the Third Workshop on Abusive Language Online* (2019, August): 19–24.
18. Stoop, W., Kunneman, F., van den Bosch, A., and Miller, B. "Detecting Harassment in Real-Time as Conversations Develop."

In *Proceedings of the Third Workshop on Abusive Language Online* (2019, August): 19–24.

19. See Zheng, Q., Xu, S., Wang, L., Tang, Y., Salvi, R. C., Freeman, G., and Huang, Y. "Understanding Safety Risks and Safety Design in Social VR Environments." *Proceedings of the ACM on Human-Computer Interaction* 7(CSCW1) (2023): 1–37; Fiani, C., Bretin, R., McGill, M., and Khamis, M. "Big Buddy: Exploring Child Reactions and Parental Perceptions Towards a Simulated Embodied Moderating System for Social Virtual Reality." In *Proceedings of the 22nd Annual ACM Interaction Design and Children Conference* (2023, June): 1–13.
20. For a recent review, see Buck, L. E., Chakraborty, S., and Bodenheimer, B. "The Impact of Embodiment and Avatar Sizing on Personal Space in Immersive Virtual Environments." *IEEE Transactions on Visualization and Computer Graphics* 28, No. 5 (2022): 2102–2113.
21. Farkas, K., Pesthy, O., Guttengéber, A., Weigl, A. S., Veres, A., Szekely, A., … Németh, D. "Altered Interpersonal Distance Regulation in Autism Spectrum Disorder." *Plos One* 18, No. 3 (2023): e0283761.
22. E.g. one (non VR) study with Chinese participants found an interpersonal distance preference that was two thirds of another study using German subjects. See Yu, X., Xiong, W., and Lee, Y. C. "An Investigation into Interpersonal and Peripersonal Spaces of Chinese People for Different Directions and Genders." *Frontiers in Psychology* 11 (2020): 981.
23. Stanton, A. "Dealing with Harassment in VR." *UploadVR*, October 25, 2016. https://www.uploadvr.com/dealing-with-harassment-in-vr/.
24. Basu, T. "The Metaverse Has a Groping Problem Already." *MIT Technology Review*, December 16, 2021. https://www.technologyreview.com/2021/12/16/1042516/the-metaverse-has-a-groping-problem.
25. Wadley, G., Carter, M., and Gibbs, M. "Voice in Virtual Worlds: The Design, Use, and Influence of Voice Chat in Online Play." *Human–Computer Interaction* 30, No. 3–4 (2015): 336–365.
26. Cote, A. C. "I Can Defend Myself": Women's Strategies for Coping with Harassment While Gaming Online." *Games and Culture* 12, No. 2 (2017): 136–155.

27. Meta. "Use Voice Mode in Meta Horizon Worlds." *Meta Quest Help*, November 2022. https://www.meta.com/en-gb/help/quest/articles/horizon/safety-and-privacy-in-horizon-worlds/use-voice-mode-horizon-worlds/.
28. Cortese, M. "Designing Safer Social VR." *Immerse*, November 2019. https://immerse.news/designing-safer-social-vr-76f99f0be82e.
29. Meta, "Personal Space in Meta Horizon Worlds." *Meta Quest Help*, December 2022. https://www.meta.com/en-gb/help/quest/articles/horizon/explore-horizon-worlds/personal-space-in-meta-horizon-worlds/.

CHAPTER 7

Regulating Social VR: Limitations and Tensions in Global Policy and Governance

Abstract This chapter investigates the evolving landscape of regulatory measures for social VR platforms, emphasising the need for government intervention to ensure that these environments are safe, trustworthy and equitable. It discusses a variety of regulatory approaches, from soft law proposals to best practice principles and industry codes of conduct, highlighting the collaborative efforts of civil society groups, government and industry stakeholders. The chapter examines global regulatory discussions, including online safety laws, data regulation and the protection of children in VR, and critiques existing self-governance initiatives. By advocating for proactive regulatory and governance interventions, this chapter highlights the necessity of placing obligations on platforms to prevent harms and protect the public interest as VR technologies continue to evolve.

Keywords Social VR regulation · Government intervention · Online safety laws · Data protection · Child safety in VR

J. E. Gray et al., *Governing Social Virtual Reality*,
https://doi.org/10.1007/978-3-031-61831-4_7

Introduction

In this chapter, we provide an overview of the current state of VR regulation, including those relating to online harms, children and data. The chapter begins with a survey of regulatory discussions concerning social VR from around the world. As our focus in this book is on social VR, we only briefly attend to the regulatory issues of competition (specifically the high-profile antitrust cases in the XR industries in Germany and the United States) and commercialisation (including sizeable government investments aimed at growing regional and national XR industries in Asia and Europe).[1] Instead, the chapter focuses on the major areas of regulatory concern relevant to harms in social VR: the governance and regulation of VR data, online safety laws and the regulation of children's use of VR. We also offer some reflections on the key limitations and issues in XR regulation today. We argue that the trend towards placing obligations on platforms to prevent, rather than respond to, harms should be extended to social VR.

In our view, we must not leave social VR governance to industry actors alone. Existing self-governance initiatives—such as Meta's recent funding of policy and research through its *XR Programs and Research Fund*[2] or the company's internal principles for 'responsible innovation'[3]—can serve to generate goodwill and support for the development of XR, but they are insufficient for protecting the public interest as VR technologies evolve.

VR Innovation, Responsibility and Safety—Global Regulatory Discussions

In regions around the world—including China,[4] Indonesia,[5] Japan,[6] France[7] and the EU—VR policy dialogues and initiatives have tended to centre on the question of how best to leverage the transition to a more immersive society for national economic gain. For instance, in 2023, the European Commission hosted a 'citizen's panel' on the topic of virtual worlds, with the aim of developing recommendations to support the region's responsible commercialisation of research and innovation objectives.[8] The consultation was followed by the introduction of an EU strategy for Web 4.0 and virtual worlds. The strategy focuses on supporting regional skills development, firms and industries, and establishing standards to support interoperability and competition. These types of policy discussions prioritise macro-level strategies for facilitating and capturing the benefits of a transition towards a more immersive digital economy. Yet, we can expect other governance issues to become increasingly salient to policymakers as the XR industry evolves. Notably, a 2022 briefing to the European Parliament explicitly raised the question of the applicability of the *Digital Services Act* and the *Artificial Intelligence Act* to developers and businesses within 'the metaverse'.[9] The briefing was critical of self-regulation by firms and raised the possibility of future regulation aimed at better equipping EU authorities to identify and respond to harmful content and conduct in immersive environments.

In South Korea in 2022, the Ministry of Science published ethical guidelines for participating in 'the metaverse'.[10] These guidelines espouse three core values: safe enjoyment, the preservation of self-identity and sustainable prosperity. To uphold these values, the guidelines suggest that participants in the metaverse should be led by the principles of authenticity, autonomy, reciprocity, respect for privacy, fairness, data protection, inclusion and responsibility. This intervention by the South Korean government may have been propelled, in part, by a number of media reports about harms occurring in VR spaces. For example, in 2021, police in South Korea reported that an adult had coerced a minor into sharing explicit photos in exchange for in-game items.[11] In another case, a minor was reportedly coerced into undressing her avatar and simulating sexual acts.[12] These types of incidents, particularly as they involve minors, highlight to policymakers the types of harms that can occur in social VR and they put pressure on lawmakers to act.

In 2022, the UK government took an important first step towards adding VR to its digital policy agenda. At a metaverse regulation symposium hosted by the Digital Regulation Cooperation Forum—with members including the UK's Competition and Markets Authority, the Information Commissioner's Office, the Office of Communications and the Financial Conduct Authority—regulators identified safety, privacy, consumer protections and competition as critical issues. During the event, there were calls for implementing safety by design obligations and embedding a duty of care approach to online safety in VR environments. The group flagged that they expect the UK's *Online Safety Bill* (discussed further below) to play an important role in establishing VR safety regulations.[13]

The Governance and Regulation of VR Data

Research shows that issues relating to VR data and user privacy are key concerns for policymakers who have begun to consider whether VR data practices fall within or without existing legal regimes.[14] For example, a 2022 European Parliament report outlining the 'risks and opportunities' of the metaverse noted that "the huge volume of data used in the metaverse raises a number of data protection and cybersecurity issues",[15] and that VR data includes "biometric data and data on the emotional and physiological responses of users, representing sensitive personal data under the GDPR [General Data Protection Regulation] and thus requiring special attention and explicit user consent for each purpose for which data is used".[16] In Australia, the Human Rights Commissioner cited VR as an example of the wider problem of networked and data-driven Internet or Things (IoT) and smart devices. Data privacy has likewise emerged as a concern for civil society groups, such as X Reality Safety Intelligence (XRSI), a US-based organisation that describes itself as "proactively anticipating and addressing the cybersecurity challenges" associated with XR, and the Future of Privacy Forum, an American data privacy advocacy group. These organisations have identified gaps in existing data privacy regimes that have implications for the XR industry. They argue that whilst XR data would fall under GDPR definitions of biometric data, US state-based privacy laws are more limited. For example, the Illinois Biometric Information Privacy Act "applies to information based on 'scans' of hand or face geometry, retinas or irises, and voiceprints, and does not explicitly cover the collection of behavioural characteristics or eye tracking".

Another regulatory lens through which to think about XR data is through the purview of competition laws. For example, in 2022, the Federal Trade Commission (FTC) in the United States attempted to block Meta's acquisition of VR fitness software developer Within,[17] only for Meta to win the federal court case the following year. Elsewhere, Germany's competition regulator, the *Bundeskartellamt,* alleged that Meta breached national data-coupling laws by tying Oculus accounts to Facebook profiles, adding to Meta's extensive first-party data collection.[18] This came on the heels of a 2019 *Bundeskartellamt* investigation into Meta's data-sharing practices.[19] Where the remit of competition regulators is consumer welfare and maintaining fair and healthy markets, the *Bundeskartellamt* has demonstrated that it understands that the accumulation and operationalisation of data are a means for large technology firms to wield market power. As FTC Chair Lina Khan puts it, there is a need for regulators to impose 'prophylactic limits'[20] on vertical integration within the tech sector to prevent the risk of tech firms broadening and deepening their data advantages.

Safety Regulations

Recently, online safety has risen to the fore as a pressing policy issue worldwide. A clear sign of this growing global concern was demonstrated at the G7 summit in 2021. The governments of the UK, Canada, France, Germany, Italy, Japan, the United States and the European Union all signed a Joint Ministerial Declaration that set forth principles designed to guide member nations' efforts in improving online safety. To date, only a handful of jurisdictions have enacted legislation, but the collective commitment suggests that more are likely to be introduced in the coming years.

Australia was one of the first jurisdictions to enact strengthened online safety laws through its *Online Safety Act* introduced in 2021. This legislation empowers Australia's eSafety Commission to (amongst other things) enforce a set of Basic Online Safety Expectations applicable to online service providers across a wide array of services and issues. These 'expectations' aim to prompt online service providers to act to *prevent* harm. The eSafety Commissioner explains that it expects service providers to:

> Take reasonable steps to be safe for their users. We expect them to minimise bullying, abuse and other harmful activity and content. We expect them to have clear and easy-to-follow ways for people to lodge complaints about unacceptable use.[21]

Whilst the Australian legislation provides some examples of what 'reasonable steps' might entail, it does not offer an exhaustive list or mandate specific requirements. Instead, service providers can collaborate with the eSafety Commission to devise steps tailored to match their business model. A pivotal development presented by this Bill is the expectation set by the Australian government for online service providers that in addition to responding reactively to harmful content, they must implement measures for proactively providing Australian citizens a baseline level of protection from harm.

The UK's *Online Safety Bill* enacted in 2023 goes further than the Australian legislation in terms of mandating platforms' obligations to proactively safeguard their users. Put simply, the UK law imposes a duty of care on online service providers requiring them to conduct comprehensive risk assessments for different age groups and take appropriate action to protect against both illegal and lawful yet harmful materials. Companies will bear additional responsibilities when their services are likely to be accessed by children. We can expect that this duty of care model will provide a powerful precedent for jurisdictions around the world seeking to impose on platforms stronger obligations to proactively protect people from harm online.

Whilst regulators and policymakers have begun to prioritise online safety more broadly, there has also been a growing recognition of the need for targeted regulation specifically addressing XR technologies. As one European Parliament document notes, XR's potential for social harm is especially problematic given the immersive affordances of XR (the potential that this content may 'feel more real'). Notably, Australia's eSafety Commission has also developed education-focused initiatives aimed at empowering users with the knowledge and skills to navigate XR responsibly. This multidimensional regulatory approach represents a promising model for proactively preventing harms posed by an emerging technology.

Regulating to Protect Children in VR

Recently, media scrutiny has intensified on the issue of harassment in social VR, especially sexual harassment directed at minors. These trends signal a future where social VR platforms will be expected to proactively shield underage users. As privacy lawyer Delara Derakshani notes, relying on users, especially children, to report adverse experiences is inadequate—the onus should be on platforms to prevent potential trauma before it occurs.[22] A range of recent regulatory initiatives support this position. As noted above, the *UK Online Safety Bill* features requirements directed at protecting young users, including obligations to prevent harmful content from appearing to under-18 users. The *European Commission's 2022 Strategy for a Better Internet for Kids* (BIK +) is underpinned by the principle that children and young people should be protected and empowered online, and this strategy is informing the development of an *EU*

Code of Conduct for Age-Appropriate Design.[23] In the United States, there have been growing calls for the Federal Communications Commission to establish regulations that would enforce the XR industry's prior position of not recommending immersive media for children under 13 until it is proven safe.[24] The bipartisan *Kids Online Safety Act*, reintroduced by the Biden Administration in the United States in 2023, would also impose a duty of care on platforms to safeguard minors from online harms.[25] As well, proposed updates to the United States' *Children's Online Privacy Protection Act* seek to establish a legal duty for platforms to prevent harms and provide better systems for parental oversight (amongst other things).

We can also expect to see policy interventions aimed at regulating the collection and use of data generated about children by VR systems and devices. In their report on children's use of VR, Common Sense Media highlighted the importance of improving privacy notices and data collection practices for child users of VR.[26] A related regulatory challenge is emerging in user-generated content platforms like *Roblox*, popular with children, where advertising is intricately woven into the game play. *Roblox's* community standards require that brands clearly and prominently disclose when content is an advertisement, and they claim not to serve advertising content to users under the age of 13. But, in 2022, the US independent advertising watchdog Truth In Advertising (TINA) filed a complaint with the FTC, arguing that "the company allows advertising to be surreptitiously interlaced with organic content",[27] for instance, in the design of what TINA describes as 'advergames': worlds, games and experiences developed by brands which feature 'stealth advertising', such as a HotWheels branded racing game. As TINA's complaint summarises, "these brands exploit unsuspecting consumers, tricking them into taking part in immersive advertising experiences".[28] This case highlights the limitations of self-regulation by platforms. Stronger legal obligations and responsibilities are required to ensure that platforms enforce their own rules to protect minors.

Limitations and Tensions in XR Regulation

As this chapter has shown, there are significant ongoing efforts on the part of regulators and policymakers globally to address the risks posed by a burgeoning global XR industry. The variety in these initiatives is indicative of an emergent policy domain in which there are a range of views about how best to approach VR governance. This variability stems in part from the fact that the industry is in such an early stage of development. Regulating emerging technology requires lawmakers to navigate the need for both technological specificity and technological agnosticism.

Technology agnostic policymaking focuses on the features and issues that most digital technologies share. From this perspective, whilst XR may intensify certain problems, these problems are known and the solutions do not look radically different to other efforts to govern digital technologies. In this view, existing governance frameworks—such as general-purpose frameworks for data protection, competition or AI—can be applied to XR, even if they do not mention the technology by name. The advantage of a technology-agnostic governance approach is that lawmakers can provide baseline rules for a space that is changing rapidly.

By contrast, technology-specific policymaking focuses attention on the novel features of a technology and the need for media-specific governance interventions. For XR, this means policymaking must be to some extent anticipatory—requiring policies that are scoped for a technology that is yet to fully form. Anticipatory governance models focus on the *future* trajectory of XR's adoption in society. There is a diachronic logic here: XR technologies *will* continue to advance and become widely adopted, and thus governance initiatives *must* be put in place proactively, pre-empting its societal impacts and its widespread entrenchment (at which point, it may be difficult to challenge or redress). This approach is of course somewhat epistemically precarious, requiring, as Nordmann[29] calls 'speculative ethics', that is the articulation of ethical concerns about emerging technologies manifesting in largely unknowable futures. For instance, whilst EU regulators are cognizant of the potential for data-related harms,[30] often regulatory discourses have been grounded in sensationalistic accounts of the 'metaverse' and as something that will require new forms of medium-specific governance, echoing the claims of novelty and innovation advanced by industry proponents.

In this book, we have viewed social VR through the lens of both technological specificity and technological agnosticism. We have identified areas where existing governance interventions can be usefully applied to social VR, but we have also called for attention to the media-specific affordances of VR, including spatiality and temporality, and the novel governance challenges it presents, such as the collection of bodily data, child safety and inclusivity. Technological specificity can be helpful for understanding the affordances of the technology as it actually exists. For social VR, this means we pay attention to the risks of acute interpersonal harm, exclusion, breaches of data privacy and so on. But specificity need not necessarily silo conversations about XR off from policy discourses relating to digital technology more broadly. An improved understanding of XR's medium-specific challenges can helpfully inform other debates about technology regulation and governance. For example, the significant attention to XR data and privacy (as an especially sensitive form of biometric and spatial data) can contribute to efforts to develop stronger restrictions on how technology companies harvest and operationalise user data across existing digital technologies.

Another key issue for XR governance is that of legitimacy. Today's industry is characterised by a high degree of industrial influence (in Western markets, much of that by a single stakeholder, Meta). Initiatives like Meta's *XR Programs and Research Fund*, through which Meta engages civil society, NGOs, industry, academia and even governments, are by design in service of economic logics and interests, operating as a mechanism through which a company mired in controversy might endear itself to the public and regulators. Whilst we are not suggesting that receiving industry funding compromises research or advocacy integrity, industrially funded initiatives to build and regulate a 'better' metaverse do shape the contours of conversations and critiques about where the harms in this emerging suite of technology are concentrated. In other words, such schemes exert a form of 'structuring power',[31] a form of boundary work demarcating what counts (and what does not) as harm and thus, where governance should be focused. To be blunt, we do not want the most powerful industry actors to pre-define what constitutes harm in social VR. Public-interest led interventions are also necessary.

Achieving good VR governance may be a complex regulatory problem but it can fit easily within the recent regulatory turn towards imposing stronger obligations on digital platforms to hold them accountable for social, economic and individual harms.[32] Our hope is that this book will lead to the inclusion of immersive technologies within scope of action taken by lawmakers around the world who are seeking to challenge the power and place of digital firms in contemporary society.

Notes

1. Egliston, B., Carter, M., and Clark, K. E. "Who Will Govern the Metaverse? Examining Governance Initiatives for Extended Reality (XR) Technologies." *New Media & Society* (2024).

2. Bosworth, A., and Clegg, N. "Building the Metaverse Responsibly" (2021). https://about.fb.com/news/2021/09/building-the-metaverse-responsibly/.
3. Applin, S., and Flick, C. "Facebook's Project Aria Indicates Problems for Responsible Innovation When Broadly Deploying AR and Other Pervasive Technology in the Commons." *Journal of Responsible Innovation* 5 (2021): 100010.
4. See, e.g., Xinhua News Agency. "China's Local Governments Double Down on Innovation to Drive Growth." *English.* www.gov.cn, February 17, 2022. http://english.www.gov.cn/news/topnews/202202/17/content_WS620e450fc6d09c94e48a5299.html.
5. See, e.g. Jiao, C., and Fathiya, D. "Indonesia Launches Own Metaverse to Promote Its Small Businesses." *Bloomberg Business*, August 1, 2022. https://www.bloomberg.com/news/articles/2022-08-01/indonesia-launches-own-metaverse-to-promote-its-small-businesses#xj4y7vzkg.
6. See, e.g., Liu, B. "Japan Gets Its Own 'Metaverse Economic Zone,' with Help from Fujitsu." *Blockworks*, February 28, 2023. https://blockworks.co/news/japan-metaverse-economic-zone.
7. Minister of Culture. "Mission Report on Metaverse Development." *Ministry of Culture France*, October 24, 2022. https://www.culture.gouv.fr/en/Documentation-space/Reports/Mission-report-on-metaverse-development.
8. Egliston, B., Carter, M., and Clark, K. E. "Who Will Govern the Metaverse? Examining Governance Initiatives for Extended Reality (XR) Technologies." *New Media & Society* (2024).
9. Tambiama, M., Car, P., Niestadt, M., and van der Pol, L. "Metaverse: Opportunities, Risks and Policy Implications." *European Parliament Research Service*, June 2022. https://www.europarl.europa.eu/RegData/etudes/BRIE/2022/733557/EPRS_BRI(2022)733557_EN.pdf.
10. Park, D. "S. Korea's Science Ministry Announces Ethical Principles for the Metaverse." *Yahoo! Finance*, August 29, 2022. https://finance.yahoo.com/news/korea-science-ministry-announces-ethical-044143407.html.
11. Park, D. "South Korea Struggles to Prevent Sexual Harassment of Minors in the Metaverse." *Forkast+*, February 18, 2022. https://forkast.news/south-korea-sexual-harassment-minors-metaverse/.

12. Camber, R. "British Police Probe VIRTUAL Rape in Metaverse: Young Girl's Digital Persona 'Is Sexually Attacked by Gang of Adult Men in Immersive Video Game'—Sparking First Investigation of Its Kind and Questions About Extent Current Laws Apply in Online World." *Daily Mail*, January 2, 2024. https://www.dailymail.co.uk/news/article-12917329/Police-launch-investigation-kind-virtual-rape-metaverse.html.
13. Howe, J. "The Metaverse and Immersive Technology—A Regulatory Perspective." *Competition and Markets Authority*, June 22, 2022. https://competitionandmarkets.blog.gov.uk/2022/06/22/the-metaverse-and-immersive-technologies-a-regulatory-perspective/; Digital Catapult. "The Meteoric Rise of the Metaverse: How Can Government and Industry Regulate It?" *Digital Catapult*, July 22, 2022. https://www.digicatapult.org.uk/expertise/blogs/post/the-meteoric-rise-of-the-metaverse-how-can-government-and-industry-regulate-it/.
14. Egliston, B., Carter, M., and Clark, K. E. "Who Will Govern the Metaverse? Examining Governance Initiatives for Extended Reality (XR) Technologies." *New Media & Society* (2024).
15. Tambiama, M., Car, P., Niestadt, M. and van der Pol, L. "Metaverse: Opportunities, Risks and Policy Implications." *European Parliament Research Service*, June 2022. https://www.europarl.europa.eu/RegData/etudes/BRIE/2022/733557/EPRS_BRI(2022)733557_EN.pdf.
16. Ibid.
17. Federal Trade Commission. "FTC Seeks to Block Virtual Reality Giant Meta's Acquisition of Popular App Creator Within." *FTC*, July 27, 2022. https://www.ftc.gov/news-events/news/press-releases/2022/07/ftc-seeks-block-virtual-reality-giant-metas-acquisition-popular-app-creator-within.
18. Bundeskartellamt. "Meta (Facebook) Responds to the Bundeskartellamt's Concerns—VR Headsets Can Now Be Used Without a Facebook Account." *Internationale Kartellkonferenz*, November 23, 2022. https://www.internationale-kartellkonferenz.de/SharedDocs/Meldung/EN/Pressemitteilungen/2022/23_11_2022_Facebook_Oculus.html.
19. Bundeskartellamt. "Bundeskartellamt Prohibits Facebook from Combining User Data from Different Sources." *Bundeskartellamt*,

February 7, 2019. https://www.bundeskartellamt.de/SharedDocs/Meldung/EN/Pressemitteilungen/2019/07_02_2019_Facebook.html.
20. Khan, L. "Amazon's Antitrust Paradox." *Yale Law Journal* 126, No. 3 (2024): 710–805.
21. eSafety Commissioner. "Learn About the Online Safety Act." *eSafety Office*. https://www.esafety.gov.au/newsroom/whats-on/online-safety-act.
22. Ryan-Mosely, T. "How an Undercover Content Moderator Polices the Metaverse." *MIT Technology Review*, April 28, 2023. https://www.technologyreview.com/2023/04/28/1072393/undercover-content-moderator-polices-the-metaverse/.
23. European Commission. "Crafting of the Code of Conduct on Age-Appropriate Design Kicks Off Today." European Commission, July 13, 2023. https://digital-strategy.ec.europa.eu/en/news/crafting-code-conduct-age-appropriate-design-kicks-today.
24. Sobel, K. *Immersive Media and Child Development: Synthesis of a Cross-Sectoral Meeting on Virtual, Augmented, and Mixed Reality and Young Children*. New York: The Joan Ganz Cooney Center at Sesame Workshop, 2019.
25. Blackburn, M. "Blackburn, Blumethal Introduce Bipartisan Kids Online Safety Act." *Blackburn.senate.gov*, May 2, 2023. https://www.blackburn.senate.gov/2023/5/blackburn-blumenthal-introduce-bipartisan-kids-online-safety-act.
26. Jerome, J. "Safe and Secure VR: Policy Issues Impacting Kids' Use of Immersive Tech." *Common Sense Media*, 2021. https://www.commonsensemedia.org/sites/default/files/featured-content/files/safe_and_secure_vr_policy_issues_impacting_kids_final.pdf.
27. Roblox. *Truth in Advertising*. Accessed July 20, 2023. https://truthinadvertising.org/brands/roblox/.
28. Smith, L., and Patten, B. "Complaint to FTC re. Roblox." *Truth in Advertising*, April 19, 2022. https://truthinadvertising.org/wp-content/uploads/2022/04/4_19_22-Complaint-to-FTC-re-Roblox.pdf.
29. Nordmann, A. "If and Then: A Critique of Speculative Nanoethics." *NanoEthics* 1, No. 31 (2007): 31–46; Nordmann, A. "Responsible Innovation, the Art and Craft of Anticipation." *Journal of Responsible Innovation* 1, No. 1 (2014): 87–98.

30. Madiega, T., Car, P. Niestadt, M., and van der Pol, L. "Metaverse: Opportunities, Risks and Policy Implications." *European Parliament Research Service* (2022).
31. Phan, T., Goldenfein, J., Kuch, D., and Mann, M. "Introduction: Economies of Virtue." In *Economies of Virtue: The Circulation of 'Ethics' in AI*, ed. T. Phan, J. Goldenfein, D. Kuch, and M. Mann (Amsterdam, NL: INC Theory on Demand, 2022), 6–23.
32. Flew, T. "The Return of the Regulatory State: Nation-States as Policy Actors in Digital Platform Governance." In *Global Communication Governance at the Crossroads* (Cham: Springer International Publishing, 2023), 161–178.

CHAPTER 8

Conclusion

Abstract This chapter synthesises the book's exploration of social VR platform governance, advocating for inclusive immersive environments in which the rights and needs of all participants are respected. It presents five key principles essential for achieving this goal: promoting pro-social cultures; prioritising prevention over reaction; embedding safety by design; ensuring user control and choice; and upholding platform responsibility and accountability. Whilst the rapid evolution of social VR presents barriers to immediate regulatory and policy interventions, the proposed principles offer a durable framework for addressing social VR's governance challenges as the technology evolves, aimed at guiding regulators, policymakers and platforms towards safer and more inclusive virtual spaces.

Keywords Social VR governance · Pro-social cultures · Safety by design · Regulatory challenges · Inclusive virtual environments

In this book, we have highlighted the ways in which social VR embodies power relations, values and practices that may entrench inequity and harm. Echoing tenets of feminist critiques of VR and notions of virtuality,[1] we have outlined how thinking about the future of social VR

J. E. Gray et al., *Governing Social Virtual Reality*,
https://doi.org/10.1007/978-3-031-61831-4_8

governance requires us to take seriously how this technology is developing and used, including how it might benefit some and not others. In so doing, we have sought to define a pathway towards social VR platform governance that nurtures safe and inclusive immersive spaces, in which the rights and needs of all participants are respected.

Based on the analysis provided in this book, we provide the following five principles as the foundation for this approach.

> ***Promote Pro-social Cultures***: Platforms should focus on preventing and minimising antisocial behaviour, and not just explicit violations of community guidelines. This includes implementing community guidelines and enforcement measures that foster a culture of compliance.
> ***Be Proactive, Not Reactive***: As content and conduct in VR are synchronous and the emotional impact potentially heightened, proactive tools for protecting users from harm should be prioritised. In social VR, reactive safety features are insufficient as they place a burden on victims to act after the harm has occurred.
> ***Safety by Natural Design***: Because VR is synchronous—and users often seek access to moderation tools when distressed—platform safety mechanisms must be designed so that they are easy and quick to access and naturally intuitive to activate.
> ***Control and Choice***: VR platforms should not assume that safety features can be configured for one type of user: what is safe and accessible for one, may not be for others. Platforms should provide a maximum amount of control and flexibility over the configuration of devices and features to ensure that experiences are inclusive of diverse users.
> ***Responsibility and Accountability***: Social VR platforms should have a legal responsibility to prevent social and individual harms. Lawmakers should develop and/or apply online safety regimes that place a responsibility on platforms to take reasonable steps to proactively protect users from harm and make platforms accountable when they fail to do so.

Social VR is a rapidly changing landscape. As we put the finishing touches on this manuscript, Apple has just released its *Vision Pro*, a 'spatial computing' device with both VR and AR capabilities. Whilst it is only available in the United States at time of writing, Apple reportedly sold close to 200,000 devices in the first few days of sales (for a hefty USD$3500 per unit) and social media has been populated with heavily mocked viral moments of YouTube content creators and tech influencers using their devices in shopping mall food courts, on the subway, when crossing the road and even whilst driving. We would not bet against these types of occurrences moving from absurdity to the everyday.

The pace of rapid change in the XR landscape is certainly a challenge for those interested in achieving good social VR governance. We are always torn between the transient, fleeting harms of the present moment; a multiverse of possible XR futures laid out by tech boosters; the very real possibility XR will not reach its expected potential (à la Google Glass) and governance efforts are wasted (or, more problematically, they lend legitimacy to the claims of XR's boosters); and the lack of knowledge about the technology, its issues and effects on users. Governance scholarship—in short—can form the basis for what Lee Vinsel calls 'criti-hype'[2]—a tendency amongst scholars to form critical stances on technology premised on speculative and outlandish future visions, with the critique providing these visions credibility and legitimacy. Indeed, it is increasingly difficult to reconcile narratives of social VR as a new infrastructure for life with the on-the-ground realities of the technology which features legless avatars, low-fidelity videoconferencing software and headsets that cause nausea. In this way, to speak of governing VR is a discursive move, one that makes a technology of the distant future feel more present.

This is why, in writing about social VR governance, we have tried to focus on where actual harms lie—this book has focused on VR governance in the context of social and interpersonal harms. Beyond this, there is a need for research and action on other issues, such as market competition and cultural policy. Whilst beyond the scope of this book, we also note recent cases of independent governance happening from 'below'. For example, we might think of technical interventions by 'ethical hackers'[3] to wrest the technological infrastructures of XR from industry, or the recalcitrant voices within industry who push back against troubling forms of XR development.[4] Future work will also need to take a critical perspective towards how the tech industry may use governance as a tool to further consolidate and wield its power. At present, in Western economies, this has largely been by Meta who, between 2021 and 2023, financed 50 million USD worth of policy and academic outreach in an attempt to "build a better metaverse".[5] Some critics have framed this initiatives as a cynical effort to drum up goodwill[6] and as a way for Meta to transmute its economic capital to cultural and political capital, protecting itself from adverse regulatory or policy intervention.

This short book has been our attempt to provide an independent view of the current state of social VR and its governance challenges, and, in a clear and accessible way, provide the knowledge needed to act. As XR continues to evolve, so may the specific issues within social VR, yet we trust that the foundational principles outlined here will retain their relevance. Good governance, after all, is in everybody's interest. Not only does it enhance user experiences, but it also has the potential to support the more widespread adoption and success of XR technologies.

Notes

1. Green, N. "Disrupting the Field: Virtual Reality Technologies and 'Multisited' Ethnographic Methods." *American Behavioral Scientist* 43, No. 3 (1999): 409–421.
2. Vinsel, L. "You're Doing It Wrong: Notes on Criticism and Technology Hype." Medium, 2021. https://sts-news.medium.com/youre-doing-it-wrong-notes-on-criticism-and-technology-hype-18b08b4307e5.
3. Egliston, B., and Carter, M. "The Material Politics of Mobile Virtual Reality: Oculus, Data, and the Technics of Sensemaking." *Convergence* 28, No. 2 (2022): 595–610.
4. Lecher, C. "Microsoft Workers' Letter Demands Company Drop Army HoloLens Contract." The Verge, February 22, 2019. https://www.theverge.com/2019/2/22/18236116/microsoft-hololens-army-contract.
5. Bosworth, A., and Clegg, N. "Building the Metaverse Responsibly," 2021. https://about.fb.com/news/2021/09/building-the-metaverse-responsibly/.
6. Applin, S., and Flick, C. "Facebook's Project Aria Indicates Problems for Responsible Innovation When Broadly Deploying AR and Other Pervasive Technology in the Commons." *Journal of Responsible Innovation* 5 (2021): 100010; Harley, D. "The Promise of Beginnings: Unpacking 'Diversity' at Oculus VR." *Convergence* 29, No. 2 (2023): 417–431.

The manufacturer's authorised representative in the EU is Springer Nature Customer Service Centre GmbH, Europaplatz 3, 69115 Heidelberg, Germany. If you have any concerns regarding our products, please contact ProductSafety@springernature.com

Printed and bound by CPI Group (UK) Ltd, Croydon, CR0 4YY
01/10/2026
02225843-0002